PUBLISHED

JEWISH ENCOUNTERS

Jonathan Rosen, General Editor

Jewish Encounters is a collaboration between Schocken and Nextbook, a project devoted to the promotion of Jewish literature, culture, and ideas.

FORTHCOMING

Resurrecting Hebrew

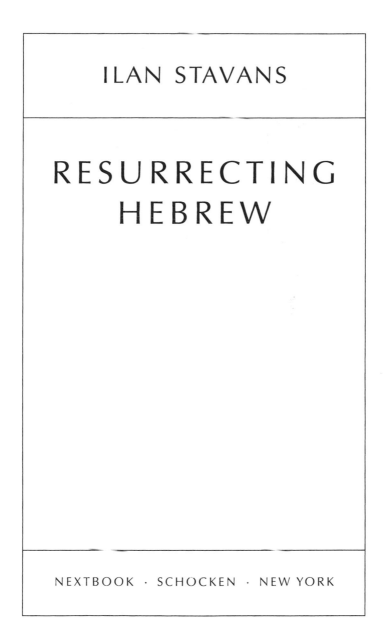

ILAN STAVANS

RESURRECTING HEBREW

NEXTBOOK · SCHOCKEN · NEW YORK

Schocken Books and colophon are registered trademarks of
Random House, Inc.

Frontispiece photo: *Eliezer Ben Yehuda* (1912),
by Yaacov Ben-Dov, The Israel Museum, Jerusalem.
Purchased with the help of Rena (Fisch) and Robert Lewin,
London. Photo © The Israel Museum by Yaacov Ben-Dov.

Owing to limitations of space, all acknowledgments to reprint
previously published and unpublished material may
be found at the end of the volume.

Library of Congress Cataloging-in-Publication Data
Stavans, Ilan.
    Resurrecting Hebrew / Ilan Stavans.
        p. cm. — (Jewish encounters)
    Includes bibliographical references and index.
    ISBN: 978-0-8052-4231-7
    1. Hebrew language—Revival.   2. Stavans, Ilan—Travel—
Israel.   3. Israel—Description and travel.   4. Ben-Yehuda,
Eliezer, 1858–1922.   I. Title.
                    PJ4551.S73 2008
                    492.409—dc22
                    2008002285

www.schocken.com
Printed in the United States of America
First Edition
2 4 6 8 9 7 5 3 1

To Halina Rubinstein
MY FOURTH-GRADE HEBREW TEACHER AT
DER YIDISHE SHULE IN MEXIQUE,
gracias AND *be'ahavah*

Hebrew was the language which the lips of the first speaker formed.

—DANTE, *De vulgari eloquentia* (1304)

CONTENTS

Resurrecting Hebrew

א

Some years ago I had the first of two dreams that pushed me
to an unexpected search, the way dreams are sometimes able
to do.

In that dream I was at a dinner party in an elegant apartment. I had never been there before. One of the hosts had
invited me, but when she opened the door and greeted me, I
realized she had forgotten my name. She stuttered while trying to recall it, to no avail. She then apologized. I told her
not to worry; I, too, have trouble remembering names.
Thankfully, I never forget my own name, at least not yet, I
said as I told it to her.

The host smiled and walked me into the living room.
There were about a dozen people in the apartment, none of
whom I knew. As I often do at parties, I got a glass of wine,
found a comfortable chair, and sat down to observe.

A voluptuous young woman with curly hair, holding a
plate of hors d'oeuvres, walked toward me. She took a seat
by my side and began an enthralling tale about an ugly, menacing beast she had seen at the zoo. The name of the beast
sounded like the *Liwerant*. She repeated the word several
times as if I knew what it meant. She said it was a fanciful,

long-necked bird with a multicolored tail that fans out like a rainbow. The beast resembled a tall turkey, with a head so small it could pass for a tennis ball and a double chin that dangled bizarrely under the long beak. Those who crossed its path swore that its penetrating eyes could frighten even a cobra. Its legs, ending in three claws, looked like pencils. And although it couldn't fly because of its meager wings, the wind could lift the beast so that it hovered overhead as if suspended by invisible strings.

"Strange," I said.

"It sings some perplexing tunes," she whispered. "And it feeds on *yarmelakis.*"

I asked her what a *yarmelaki* was, but she ignored my question.

I suddenly realized that *yarmelaki* wasn't the only word I hadn't understood. As she spun her yarn, it became increasingly difficult to follow her sentences. She seemed to be speaking in a foreign language.

I was completely at a loss. Was she still talking about the *Liwerant?*

I felt uncomfortable and looked around. I saw a cadre of rabbis. One of them resembled a great-grandfather of mine, Kalman Eisenberg, whose sepia photograph, given to me by my mother, hangs in the ground-floor hallway of my house. The other rabbis looked like what Kalman Eisenberg's friends probably looked like. I told the woman I needed fresh air and headed in the direction of the rabbis, who, I believe, were conferring about a Talmudic passage—something about an apple falling from a tree into the yard on a neighbor's side of the fence. "Does the apple belong to the owner of the tree, or is it now the neighbor's property?" asked one of the rabbis.

Since dreams allow for dead people to come visit, I asked Great-grandfather Kalman if he knew what language the attractive woman spoke. He looked at me in disbelief. "But of course," he replied. "It's Hebrew. She's my niece."

"It can't be," I replied. "I know Hebrew."

"You do?" he questioned. "Then you must be aware that God doesn't act alone. He is perpetually in need of help."

I looked toward the chair where the beautiful woman had been sitting. To my surprise, she had taken off her clothes. She must have been in her early thirties, but her short, curly black hair made her look younger. Her beauty was stunning.

The woman was sitting next to a rabbi. In the dream it crossed my mind that such a scene was utterly impossible. Rabbis aren't allowed to be with women who aren't their spouses, let alone naked ones.

At this point I woke up in a cold sweat. My teeth were chattering.

Dreams can refer to unfinished business we might have, people we're in debt to, journeys we're ready to embark on. They have something to say to us, something that reason alone cannot explain.

The Talmud says that an uninterpreted dream is like an unread letter.

I spent weeks trying to sort out my dream. The face of the woman wasn't recognizable to me. I couldn't remember having thought about Kalman Eisenberg in the preceding weeks. Maybe the act of simply walking back and forth through the ground-floor hallway had brought his image into my unconscious. I still didn't know what a *yarmelaki* was. Could it be an echo of the Yiddish word for head covering? The presence of the *Liwerant* was easier for me to explain. Not that I had ever seen such an anomalous creature, but recently I had become interested in imaginary animals and, as a result, had acquired an old copy of *The First Voyage Round the World*, by Magellan, an 1874 edition translated by Lord Stanley of Alderley, about imaginary kingdoms. It contained references to a couple of beautiful dead birds from "the terrestrial Paradise" called *Bolom Niwatha*. The birds were said to be "large as thrushes, [with] small heads, long beaks, legs slender like a writing pen, and a span in length." Instead of wings, they have "long feathers of different colours, like plumes. . . . They never fly, except when the wind blows."

I had been intrigued by these curious animals, but it wasn't the *Liwerant* I was most attracted to. The part of the dream that kept coming back to my mind involved the unintelligible woman. Was it really Hebrew she was speaking? How come I couldn't understand her? Why did she undress? And how to explain the reference to God needing help?

Several months later, I told a friend who has known me for decades about the dream. I described it to him in detail. His response was unexpected.

"Have you forgotten your Hebrew?" he asked.

"Why?" I didn't have much to say. "Maybe I have. There was once a time when I could speak it fluently. But I haven't used it for years." I paused. "Yes, I have abandoned it."

He said that I was going through a period of language withdrawal.

I had never heard the expression *language withdrawal* before, yet I immediately felt guilty.

My friend said, "Losing one's Hebrew might be a synonym for losing one's soul."

ב

A week later, I received in the mail from this friend a used copy of *A Dream Come True*, the autobiography of Eliezer Ben-Yehuda. With it came a succinct note: "Ilan, your dream about the strange bird with the long beak? It could have been dreamt by Ben-Yehuda. Do you know what *Eliezer* means in Hebrew? My God has helped."

The name Eliezer Ben-Yehuda was familiar to me. In my youth I had read about how the Lithuanian-born lexicographer had devoted his life to a single mission: to revive the three-thousand-year-old biblical language, to adapt it to the modern world by making it a centerpiece of Zionism, the movement that began in the nineteenth century to create a state for the dispersed Jewish people.

So I delved into the book. I didn't find Ben-Yehuda's writing inspiring. His style was careless, repetitive, and indistinguishable from a standard nineteenth-century autobiography of a colonial in the British Empire. He might have been a Zionist icon, but in his writing—at least in *A Dream Come True*—he was rather unsophisticated. The book is a narrative of his life from the moment he discovered "the fire of love for the Hebrew language" up to 1882, the year when, having settled in Jerusalem, his son Ben-Zion Ben-Yehuda, described as the first child in modern times to speak Hebrew, was born. (Ben-Zion Ben-Yehuda, later called Itamar Ben-Avi, would grow up to become an important Hebrew journalist.) It's clearly a patch job, pulled together from installments Ben-Yehuda published in Hebrew in the periodical *Ha-Toren* from December 1917 through December 1918.

Ben-Yehuda's writing may have disappointed me, but I was hooked. My friend had sensed an inner disquiet in my response to his question about losing my Hebrew.

I was overwhelmed by a desire to reclaim the language, not only as a skill—to communicate with others in it, to live with it, to be inhabited by it—but to find out everything I could about its history.

I had learned my Hebrew as a child at the Yidishe Shule, the Bundist day school I attended in Mexico City. The school was decidedly secular. Our heroes were luminaries like Sholem Aleichem, Marc Chagall, and Mordecai Anielewicz, representatives of Yiddish civilization in the world into which Eliezer Ben-Yehuda was born. The education I received was built on the idea of difference. As Mexican Jews, we were told we were unique because of our millenarian journey across the globe. We were Mexicans because our forebears had immigrated to that country from the Pale of Settlement. Most important, we were Jews. And being Jewish meant being somewhat abnormal, not in the psychological sense but in the political one. Many of us disliked this message. We fought to be like everyone else. But, as a teacher of mine once said to me, it is precisely our desire to be like everyone else that makes us different.

I still remember my second-grade teacher writing on the blackboard the twenty-two letters of the Hebrew alphabet, which she used to introduce us to the multifaceted world of *Yiddishkeit*. She explained them by means of music. The class sang for most of the session a number of different songs. The one that stuck in my mind is the lullaby *"Oyfn Pripetchik"* (in English, "At the Fireplace"). Originally titled *"Der alef-beys,"* it was composed by Mark Varshavsky, whose compilation *Yiddish Folk Songs* was published in 1900. Steven Spielberg used the song—to my taste in a saccharine fashion—in his film *Schindler's List*. In English, it reads:

A flame burns in the fireplace,
the room warms up,
as the teacher drills the children
in the *alef-beys.*

"Remember dear children
what you are learning here.
Repeat it again and again:
kometz-alef is pronounced *o.*

When you grow older
you will understand
that this alphabet contains
the tears and the weeping of our people.

When you grow weary
and burdened with exile,
You will find comfort and strength
within the Jewish alphabet."

Once the singing had ended, we would talk about the letters one by one: about *aleph*, *bet*, *gimel*, *dalet* . . . The teacher would ask us to come up with a word starting with another letter. I remember her telling me once: "Ilan, you're a lucky boy. Your name starts with *aleph*, the first letter of the alphabet."

When I did further research, I found out that *"Oyfn Pripetchik"* was popular, in part, because of the discovery of Varshavsky's work by the Yiddish litterateur Sholem Aleichem, author of the classic *Tevye the Dairyman*, on which the Broadway musical *Fiddler on the Roof* was based. During the Holocaust, the lullaby was turned into a ghetto song, with the following modified line: "At the ghetto wall a fire burns, the surveillance is keen." In the Soviet Union in the sixties, it was a clandestine tune. But in the Mexico of my childhood, it was a portal to the Yiddish alphabet. It wasn't the Hebrew letters that the teacher was teaching us, but the *alef-beys*. Our Bundist forebears, methodical in their hatred of religion, were biased supporters of the *mame-loshn* in the language wars that since the *Haskalah*, or Jewish Enlightenment, had divided the Jewish people between secularists and their enemies, the Orthodox. They wanted to elevate Sholem Aleichem's tongue to new heights. They wanted us to be a link to its future.

Hostility toward Hebrew began to diminish when I was in my teens. Among Mexican Jews, the seventies were a period in which Zionism, as an ideology, made a dent in our consciousness. Israel, riding on the wave of military self-assurance that resulted from the Six-Day War, sent proselytizing emissaries to the various Jewish communities of the Diaspora, hoping to persuade youth to make aliyah—return to the Promised Land. Latin America, with the fourth-largest concentration of Jews worldwide (after the United States, the Soviet bloc, and France), was a prime target, especially Argentina, Brazil, and Mexico, where most Jews were concentrated.

Hebrew-language classes became mandatory in the Yidishe Shule. Textbooks were imported from Israel. Their Socialist images (tractors, irrigation devices, pails and shovels) were at odds with the bourgeois life Mexican Jews lived. We learned about David Ben-Gurion, the first Israeli prime minister, about the valiant one-eyed army man Moshe Dayan, about the martyred soldiers of the War of Independence. We learned about the kibbutz as the self-sustaining agricultural model of the future. And we learned about Diaspora Jews in the Middle Ages, such as Yehuda Halevi and Nahmanides, who at some point in their lives had decided to leave their country of origin to make aliyah. Some died in transit; others arrived safely, and lived and died in the Holy Land. Concomitant to our existence in the land of the Aztecs was another nation that was also ours. It was only a matter of assuming our birthright for it to grant us full-fledged citizenship. Were we ready to ascend?

Maybe.

Not only the present reality of Israel but the history of Zionism became an important part of the curriculum. In order to understand the struggles of the modern country, a constellation of Zionist thinkers was presented to us: Theodor Herzl, Moses Hess, Max Nordau, Berl Katzenelson, Ahad Ha-Am, Vladimir Jabotinsky, Chaim Weizmann, and . . . yes, Eliezer Ben-Yehuda. Like most of my friends, I learned the essentials about Ben-Yehuda. I don't remember being particularly interested in his plight, though. Herzl, a Hungarian-born journalist whose mission became clear during the Dreyfus Affair in France, was far more attractive. One of my teachers gave me segments of Herzl's 1896 manifesto, *The Jewish State*. It was arguably the most affecting piece of Zionist literature that crossed my eyes at the time.

My grandmother Bela Stavchansky was a Polish Jew who had immigrated to Mexico, where her three children were born; she was widowed in 1965. At one point she traveled to Israel and brought me back a small bottle of colored sand (yellow, orange, red, and green) from the Negev Desert as a souvenir. She told me that as soon as she descended from the airplane in Tel Aviv, she had kneeled down and kissed the ground. Every Jew from the Diaspora longs to return to the holiest of places, she said. The kiss is proof of our inner longing.

I kept the bottle on one of the shelves in my bedroom for years but seldom thought about it.

When I made my own first trip to Israel in 1979, I didn't think about kneeling and kissing the ground. Nor did I look at the sand in the desert as more significant than the sand with which I had built castles, fortresses, and other sophisticated architectural structures during summer vacations in Acapulco. Still, I had deferred my entrance to college to live in Israel for a year. Life in the Diaspora was confusing to me. What was I, a Mexican or a Jew? Did I need to choose between the two? What made me Mexican other than the accidental route my ancestors had taken to the New World from Poland and the Ukraine in the twenties?

I lived in a number of places. I spent months in Tel Katzir, a kibbutz of about four hundred people, created in 1949 near the Sea of Galilee. My tasks were multifold: I worked in the banana fields, did carpentry, milked cows and helped them to give birth to their calves, fed the ostriches, and washed dishes in the kitchen. After I left the kibbutz, I shared a small room in Yemin Moshe, the bohemian section in Jerusalem. And I spent time writing in a somber apartment in Haifa.

During that period, I fell in love with a beautiful army recruit from Petach Tikvah who was about to get married. The nights we spent together, before she was called back to her base, still linger in me.

Israel for me then was about sex and sweat. The Yom Kippur War had taken place six years earlier. Although it had been a resounding triumph from a military point of view, it had come at a terrible price, and the euphoria of the previous two decades had receded. It was becoming clear to Israelis that their Arab enemies, while incapable of casting them into the Mediterranean Sea as they repeatedly promised to do, weren't ready to renounce their hatred of the Jewish State. Furthermore, the Palestinian refugee problem was growing.

Many of my teachers at the Yidishe Shule had been Mexican women who had learned Hebrew in *ulpans*, intensive Hebrew-language programs. But I also had some *shlichim*, pedagogical envoys from Israel the school had hired to bring the Zionist ideology to its student body. The *shlichim* told me about foresting the desert, building bunkers to protect the population from falling Katyushas, consolidating financial institutions to make the nation more solvent. They were proud of their nation, built on Socialist principles but capable of making peace with capitalism. However, their pride had a double edge. It concealed an element of condescension toward the Jews who had not returned to Israel. We were in need of redemption—still in bondage. They perceived the Diaspora as synonymous with backwardness. In their eyes, that odious psychological vulnerability needed to be eradicated.

In Israel I was eager to practice my Hebrew, to speak like a native as soon as possible. I made it a task to get the news from the newspaper *Haaretz* on a daily basis. Within a short time, I was reading writers such as Hayyim Nahman Bialik, the leading poet of the Hebrew renaissance, the Galicia-born novelist Shmuel Yosef Agnon, and the younger crop in the original.

I found scores of Jews like me—dislocated tongue-snatchers ready to make the leap to become natives.

Much as I tried, I couldn't feel fully at home. I soon realized that, deep inside, I liked being divided: Mexican *and*

Jewish. Or, more precisely, I found that the concept of difference the Yidishe Shule had instilled in me had permeated my entire identity. In the streets of Mexico I had been singled out as a Jew, making me feel uncomfortable, though not altogether unwelcome. My skin color was different, my name was different (I was born Ilan Stavchansky), my education was different. I didn't fit in . . . and I liked it.

Discomfort can be a pleasant sensation.

I left Israel in 1980. Not once in the years that followed did I think of returning there permanently as an option. Hebrew took a backseat.

A few years later, I immigrated to New York City. English became my primary language. I also became infatuated with the crossbreeding of tongues: English entering the realm of Spanish, French making inroads into Arabic, Turkish absorbing elements of German. My work as a writer appeared under the pen name Ilan Stavans. In due time, it became my persona.

For the next twenty years, Israel might have been on my mind whenever I read the news. I saw the tragedy of repeated terrorist attacks and systematic military retaliation from afar. I was comfortable in my Diasporic fishbowl.

My dream changed all that. Language withdrawal: What kind of relationship did I retain with Hebrew? Was it defined by Israel? How could one conceptualize the itinerant life of the language from prebiblical times to its contemporary incarnation? There was definitely something deeply perplexing about my relationship with the language. Had I given up on a central aspect of my identity? To what extent was I, a reluctant speaker, an integral part of the history of Hebrew? The friend to whom I had first related my dream had told me that losing one's Hebrew is like losing one's soul. Had I become soulless?

λ

I needed to gain some perspective on the development of Hebrew as an ancient language, and for this there was one friend I wanted to talk to: Angel Sáenz-Badillos.

Sáenz-Badillos lives in Cambridge, Massachusetts, where he is loosely affiliated with Harvard's exchange program in Spain. His daughter, a pediatrician, works in the area, and Sáenz-Badillos and his wife, Judit Targarona, moved there to be near her and her family. For years Sáenz-Badillos taught the history of the Hebrew language and its literature at Madrid's Universidad Complutense. Targarona is the author of a popular Hebrew-Spanish dictionary. Most important, Sáenz-Badillos is the author of an unsurpassed history of the Hebrew language, first published in Spanish in 1983.

I find it ironic that a Spaniard—and a non-Jew, for that matter—should be one of the world's authorities on the subject. Centuries ago Spain was a center of Jewish learning. But since the expulsion of Jews in 1492, the peninsula has been nearly devoid of Jewish culture. Little remains of the academies dedicated to philosophy, translation, and the exact sciences. Poetry flourished in Hebrew (inspired by

Arabic models), but today very few of the celebrated names are taught in schools. One gets the impression, upon visiting Spain these days, that the country has done everything in its power to erase its Jewish roots.

Thus, my fascination with Sáenz-Badillos. I knew that a consultation with him would enable me to get a better grasp on Hebrew.

Sáenz-Badillos was a patient guide as he walked me through the uniqueness of Hebrew in the community of tongues. As a Semitic language, Hebrew developed in the Near East, between the Jordan River and the Mediterranean Sea, in the late second and first millennia B.C.E. Among the earliest archaeological items available, the Gezer Calendar, discovered by R. A. S. Macalister in 1908 and preserved in Istanbul's Museum of Antiquities, dates from the tenth century B.C.E., the time of King David and King Solomon. Its six lines are a record of the labor connected to the construction of a tunnel at the time of King Hezekiah, mentioned in 2 Kings 20:20 and 2 Chronicles 32:3 and 33:14. This means that the language used in previous periods is, to a large extent, still unknown. A number of scholars—among them the nineteenth-century German archaeologist Hugo Winckler, who discovered the capital of the Hittite Empire—suggest that cuneiform was the system of writing used in ancient Israel. Others believe that the square Hebrew alphabet was already in use at the time when Moses supposedly lived in Egypt, orchestrating an upheaval to liberate the slaves from Pharaoh's control.

"What kind of Hebrew did you learn in Mexico?" Sáenz-Badillos asked me.

"I don't know," I replied. "How many are there?" I mentioned our singing of *"Der alef-beys"* at the Yidishe Shule.

He said that just as the English language is classified by historians into Old (the Celtic dialects spoken in Scotland, Wales, and Cornwall), Middle (from the Norman invasion in 1066 to the mid- to late fifteenth century), and Modern (Shakespeare's tongue, from the mid- to late sixteenth century on), there are at least three distinctive epochs in the evolution of Hebrew: an early period before the consolidation of Israel as a clear-cut nation, when the language was a Canaanite dialect; the language of the Davidic Kingdom, aka biblical Hebrew; and the modern version in Israel.

How different are they?

As different as the thirteenth-century poet Gonzalo de Berceo's Spanish is from that of Gabriel García Márquez in *One Hundred Years of Solitude.* Or as Chaucer's English is from that of Dickens.

Sáenz-Badillos explained: "There are historians of language who suggest that the term *Hebrew* has too many meanings and that it should be broken into subdivisions. They suggest talking of Hebrew as the biblical language and Israeli as the one used by the Zionist pioneers from Eliezer Ben-Yehuda to the present day. In any event, Hebrew is part of a canon of some seventy different languages recognized as Semitic. They share a phonology, morphology, and syntax. These languages originated in a geographical spread that spanned from Mesopotamia to the southern parts of Arabia, onward to Ethiopia and the Middle East."

Hebrew's immediate ancestor is Phoenician. Phoenician culture, with the city-states of Tyre, Sarepta, and Sidon, flourished in the Mediterranean basin in what was known as Canaan. It spread along the coast from 1200 to 900 B.C.E., reaching the area now occupied by Lebanon. Its people described themselves as *bani kan'an*, children of Canaan.

I told Sáenz-Badillos that I believed this was also the name used to describe the Israelites in Isaiah 19:18.

"Yes," he answered. "In the Bible Phoenicians are called Sidonians. It's the Greeks who named them Phoenicians. Have you ever seen a tableau of the Phoenician letters?"

"I might have come across it in the past."

The Phoenician alphabet shaped early Hebrew. It also influenced other Semitic alphabets, such as Arabic, and left its imprint on Greek, Roman, and Cyrillic as well. "The origins of Hebrew are still in question," noted Sáenz-Badillos. "It isn't known in what language the Patriarchs spoke. It is possible that when the Israelites conquered Canaan, they adopted the language of the place. The letters of Tel el-Amarna—clay tablets covered with Akkadian cuneiform found in this city on the Nile in 1887, some of which date to a period before the conquest of Canaan—correspond in historical time to roughly between 1385 and 1355 B.C.E., and show continuity between the regions of Mesopotamia, Egypt, and the land of settlement of the Canaanite tribes."

"What are the first archaeological items available?" I asked him.

Sáenz-Badillos responded that we can get a glimpse of early Hebrew script in a number of inscriptions from Judea and Samaria that appear in documents relating to taxes and supplies of oil. The letters in them appear to be related to those in other Semitic alphabets from northern Canaan.

They tend to be curved at the bottom, especially the *bet*, *qof*, *lamed*, *mem*, and *pe*. As in most early Semitic languages, words aren't separated by spaces.

He said that the alphabet became stabilized at twenty-two letters. "Strikingly, with minor stylistic changes, these letters, from *aleph* to *tav*, remain untouched to the present day. The same letters that passed through King Saul's eyes were used by the psalmists, Rabbi Akiva, Shmuel ha-Nagid, Ben-Yehuda, and David Grossman."

He continued: "But unquestionably the most astounding document in the history of Hebrew is the Five Books of Moses. These books offer a compelling story from the beginnings of Creation to the moment Abraham and his descendants are chosen by God to become a light to other nations and beyond." Sáenz-Badillos stated that the earliest material is the poetry, such as Genesis 49, Exodus 15, and Deuteronomy 32. Even though it is clear that subsequent editors have manipulated the Hebrew in these sections, it is still possible to trace influences of neighboring dialects used in the northern region of Canaan. For the most part, the prose in the Bible dates to the period of King David, when a national language appeared to have been used in Jerusalem at court and among the educated elite.

"It's important to keep in mind," emphasized Sáenz-Badillos, "that biblical Hebrew allows a glimpse of the speech used by the Israelites and a very small one at that. After all, it contains approximately eight thousand items, not even remotely close to what a living language needs to display a range of emotions. This doesn't mean that the language used for daily interaction was limited. The Torah records a portion of it. One can only guess how Hebrew sounded during David's years in power, from approximately 1011 to 971 B.C.E., as he conquered Jerusalem and made it his capital. The record of his reign (from chapter 16 onward in First Samuel, Second Samuel, First Kings, and a portion of Second Kings) was drafted much later, in a language belonging to a different period, and is part of the *Tanakh*, which goes beyond the five books attributed to Moses and includes the narratives about prophets, the books of Job and Ecclesiastes, and so on. Still, judging from the range of possibilities in the language of the Torah, it is clear that biblical Hebrew was versatile, capable of depth and complexity."

"Whenever I glance at a page of the Torah," I said, "the words appear immobile, as if they've been sitting there since the beginning of time."

"Yet you need to think of the polyphonic nature of biblical Hebrew," responded Sáenz-Badillos. "From the genealogical list in Genesis to the dietary principles in Deuteronomy and the legalistic diatribes in Leviticus, the narrative registers change. All exhibit unique authorial devices. There are also philosophical disquisitions, such as Ecclesiastes ('vanity of vanities; all *is* vanity'), and sections focusing not on a large set of characters but on a single individual put to a test, like the book of Job ('a man in the land of Uz, whose name was Job . . . [He] feared God and eschewed evil')."

As for the compilation of the Bible, Sáenz-Badillos explained: "As a canonized anthology, the Torah probably began to be compiled in the mid-fifth century B.C.E., at the request of the priestly scribe Ezra. Having led about five thousand Israelites in exile from Babylon back to their home in Jerusalem, Ezra orchestrated the editing of the five books. The process of expanding, modifying, and adjusting the text continued unabated for centuries. It also left behind material judged by the various editors to be unacceptable. These books came to be known as Apocrypha and Pseudepigrapha. The language as it appears in the Bible is in constant flux. It is possible to discern an archaic modality used until the Babylonian exile, the Hebrew used in the Babylonian exile, and a late type used between the sixth and fourth centuries B.C.E. corresponding to the Persian period."

The stabilizing of the content seems to have been completed by the second century C.E. A period of dissemination ensued. "There were people charged with transcribing and conserving the text," Sáenz-Badillos said. "Then the Masoretes, who lived between the seventh and the eleventh centuries, produced guidelines for pronunciation and grammar through diacritical marks, called *tag* (plural, *taggîn*), marking the way letters and words ought to be accented. The *taggîn* aren't letters per se. They acquire different forms, sometimes appearing as little strokes at the side, below, or above a letter. There can be letters with one stroke, two, three, and even six. The signs include the *dagesh*, *mappîq*, *raphe*, and the diacritical points on the *shin*. The *taggîn* enable today's listeners to know how Hebrew was pronounced. They make the reading of the text harmonious, enchanting, hypnotic even."

I wanted to know about the role of Aramaic in the shaping of the Bible. Sáenz-Badillos said that it was a contested question. Imperial Aramaic, the lingua franca—the equivalent of global English nowadays—evolved in the tenth century B.C.E. among a people from what is now Syria and Iraq (formerly Mesopotamia). Although as a people the Arameans never became very powerful, their tongue was widely used in western Asia from the second half of the first millennium B.C.E. onward. Traces of Aramaic have been found as far away as India. Countless loanwords, changed endings, and transformed verb tenses became standard in various Semitic languages, including Hebrew.

The interface between Aramaic and biblical Hebrew shaped the language Ezra used while codifying the Torah. The degree to which he and the cadre of scribes surrounding him were defined by a hybrid in vogue at the time is open for discussion. That linguistic tension left an imprint in Jewish literature across the ages, including a Talmudic passage in which the coexistence of Hebrew, Assyrian, and Aramaic is presented as a matter of choice for the Israelites.

Sáenz-Badillos recommended that I look up this passage. Later on, I did. It's in the Babylonian Talmud, *Sanhedrin* 21b:

> Mar Zutra or, as some say, Mar 'Uqbā said: Originally the Torah was given to Israel in Hebrew characters and in the ancient Israelite script and the Holy Tongue; it was given again to them, in the days of Ezra, in the *ketabh 'asshuri* (Assyrian writing) and in the Aramaic tongue. The Jewish people chose for themselves the Assyrian script and the Holy Tongue, and left the Israelite script and Aramaic tongue for mundane people. Who were the mundane people? Rabbi Chisda said, the Samaritans. What is the Israelite script? Rabbi Chisda adds: *Libuna'ah*.

I was puzzled by the word *Libuna'ah*. "What does it mean?" I asked Sáenz-Badillos.

"It might be taken to mean an inferior script," he told me. "The eleventh-century French exegete Rabbi Shlomo ben Yitzhak (aka Rashi) suggested it should be seen as the oversize script often used in amulets and mezuzahs. In any case, it is clear that issues of class were emphasized by their respective parlance. The elite (Kohanim and Levites) used one tongue and the masses another. The Bible was designed for the elite to read out loud to the people."

I told Sáenz-Badillos that after I had a dream about losing the Hebrew I'd learned in Mexico when I was young, a friend of mine had suggested that what I was experiencing was a symptom of language withdrawal.

"Yes, I like the diagnosis. The history of the Jewish Diaspora shows long stretches of a similar symptom. People kept Hebrew in a refrigerator."

I told Sáenz-Badillos that, as a result of my dream, I had become interested in Ben-Yehuda's odyssey. "How much of all this history of Hebrew do you know?" I asked him.

He said he wasn't a specialist in Ben-Yehuda but mentioned Ben-Yehuda's essay "A Burning Question"—"*She'elah Lohatah*" in Hebrew. He also said that although the Jews who were already living in Palestine had used Hebrew, when Ben-Yehuda immigrated in 1881 the language wasn't in common use. Each community there used its own Diasporic tongue. He said that it was the wave of immigrants from Russia who embraced the idea of transforming Hebrew into a national language as a way to renew Jewish culture.

"It was a utopian idea," Sáenz-Badillos stressed. "Imagine, for a second, that suddenly the descendants of the Romans decided to revive the language made immortal in the poetry of Catullus, Virgil, Horace, and Ovid, the satire of Juvenal, and the theater of Seneca. A desire to make it part of the present, to turn it into an ideological—that is, nationalist—drive, would need to occur, persuading people that the *Imperium Romanum*, which flourished roughly between Julius Caesar's rise to power in the first century B.C.E. and the fall of its western part in 476 C.E., ought to return today in Italy. And the drive would state that Latin, not Italian, is the true tongue."

"Impossible!"

"Indeed," said Sáenz-Badillos. Then he explained that during the first part of the revival, Ben-Yehuda had concentrated on phonology, orthography, morphology, and syntax. But the crucial aspect was the coining of new terms, which would adapt an antiquated Hebrew to modern life. To achieve this, Ben-Yehuda published his own periodical. And he began work on his magnum opus, a thesaurus. "It was a laudable project," Sáenz-Badillos affirmed, "even though about two thousand words created by him would not be embraced by the population that surrounded him. They would fall into disuse."

Sáenz-Badillos's portrait of Ben-Yehuda suggested to me a dreamer with his feet firmly on the ground.

ד

I wanted to know more about Eliezer Ben-Yehuda. How did he come to Hebrew? I sought anything I could put my hands on that was connected with him, no matter how loosely.

For Ben-Yehuda, literal and linguistic exile was an unfathomable torment. "All my life I have been inconsolably grieved about two things," he wrote in *A Dream Come True*. "I was not born in Jerusalem, not even in the land of Israel. And my speech, from the moment I was able to utter words, was not in Hebrew."

He had been born Eliezer Yitzhak Perelman into a Hasidic family in the Jewish Quarter of the small village of Luzhky. The year was 1858. The village was part of the Russian Empire ruled by Czar Alexander II. The first of eight children, Ben-Yehuda was a sickly boy diagnosed with tuberculosis at a time when the illness didn't have a cure, a fact that confined him to his home, where he became an avid reader. His father, a Habad Hasid who died when Ben-Yehuda was quite young, was an impractical man who spent time poring through books and engaging others in Talmudic discussions. Ben-Yehuda's mother was savvy and entrepreneurial. At first the couple received money from their respective parents. But when Ben-Yehuda was still young, his mother opened a small grocery store in their home to sell wax candles, flour, and other items.

What role did Hebrew play in his childhood? It was the

archaic tongue of sacred literature. It was mostly written, not spoken. The glimpse he got of the Talmudic discussions the elders engaged in confirmed to him that its oral use was limited. For the most part, these discussions were in Yiddish with a few Hebrew quotations sprinkled throughout, mostly, he would say later, "to display pompous wisdom." It was surely not a living language—but not a dead one, either.

Ben-Yehuda felt attracted to Hebrew because of its universal quality. Litvaks and Galitzianers alike, as folks from Lithuania and Galicia were known, could understand it when they read it. So could the Jews of Istanbul. The revival of Hebrew as a modern tongue wasn't exclusively the domain of Ben-Yehuda. Psalms 137:5 has always been a cornerstone in Jewish life: "If I forget thee, O Jerusalem, let my right hand forget her cunning." In antiquity, the line was recited in Alexandria, in Algiers, in Seville. The language spoken in the land, the language of the psalms, and the land it dreamed of fused into a single vision of wholeness. And so Zionism and the revival of Hebrew have been intimately connected.

The infrastructure for the revival of Hebrew began centuries before Ben-Yehuda's effort. Among the earliest modern literary manifestations was *Zahut Bedihuta de-Kiddushim*, a late-sixteenth-century play by J. Sommo. There was also the Yiddish-Hebrew dictionary by Elijah Levita, the Renaissance-period grammarian, poet, and author of the *Bove Bukh* (1507–8), the most popular chivalric romance composed in Old Yiddish. *Ha-Me'assef*, a quarterly review, appeared between 1783 and 1797, and between 1808 and 1811.

Likewise, the weekly *Ha-Maggid* began to appear in Russia in 1856. And there were Hebrew-language newspapers in Ferrara, Italy, and Dessau, Germany. Finally, Abraham Mapu's *Ahavat Tziyyon*, the first novel ever to be written in Hebrew, was released in 1853.

In modern times, the way was paved by rabbinical commentators who, while not discussing the issue directly, set the conditions for its consideration. Yehuda Alkalai from Sarajevo stated in his 1834 booklet *Shema Yisrael* that he thought it unwise to wait until God gave a sign to establish Jewish colonies in the Holy Land. He saw it as "the necessary preparation for the descent of the Divine Presence among us; afterward, He will grant us and all Israel further signs in His favor." Likewise, Zevi Hirsch Kalischer from Posen, a province in western Poland, wrote in *Derishat Tziyyon (Seeking Zion)* (1862) that "to concentrate all one's energy in the holy work and to renounce home and fortune for the sake of living in Zion before 'the voice of gladness' and 'the voice of joy' are heard—there is no greater merit or trial than this."

Naturally, the issue of returning to the Promised Land was alive long before Alkalai and Kalischer. Redemption is a Jewish concept. The Talmud (Tractate *Shabbat* 118b) states: "It is taught in the name of Rabbi Elisha ben Abuya [ca. 60–130 C.E.]: 'Everyone who dwells permanently in the land of Israel, recites the *Shema* morning and evening, and speaks the sacred tongue is assured that he will dwell in the World to Come.' " After the Babylonian exile, redemption took on a new meaning. It was no longer about devotion; the idea of return became attached to it. To live in the Promised Land *and* to speak Hebrew—therein lay redemption.

Many of the founding fathers of Zionism thought it cumbersome to teach the masses a language they perceived as fossilized. Why waste energy in such tasks? There were numerous other worthy endeavors, many believed. Theodor Herzl, a German-speaking Hungarian-born journalist and arguably the central force behind the Zionist pursuit, was himself among them. (Herzl was Ben-Yehuda's junior by two years.) In his pamphlet *The Jewish State*, which appeared in 1896, Herzl doesn't mention Hebrew as part of his nationalist project. Indeed, he envisoned German to be the language of Israel. Shortly before his death in Vienna in 1904, Herzl said: "We cannot converse with one another in Hebrew. Who amongst us has sufficient acquaintance with Hebrew to ask for a railway ticket in that language?" It was left to others to link linguistic and national resurrection.

Ben-Yehuda's embrace of secularism derived from the mix of his rebellious spirit and his gravitation toward teachers and thinkers who combined their views of orthodoxy with an interest in Western culture. Since becoming a rabbi was in his DNA, he enrolled in a yeshiva in Plotzk, which at the time was a center of Hasidic learning in Lithuania. But instead of devoting himself exclusively to rabbinical exegesis, Ben-Yehuda came across a string of teachers who introduced him to Western literature. Believing that reading secular literature could lead to a regretful life, the family sent Ben-Yehuda to Vilna, where he met Samuel Napthali Herz Jonas, who also was attracted to Enlightenment literature and ended up becoming his father-in-law. (His first marriage was to Jonas's eldest daughter, Dvora.)

Later on, when Ben-Yehuda dropped his religious studies and attended a gymnasium in Dünaburg, the Latvian commercial city on the western Dvina River, he became mesmerized by the ideological debates that surrounded him: socialism, anarchism, communism, bundism. From all of them he chose Zionism.

It is important to keep in mind that the Pale of Settlement at the time was nearly powerless. Since the Enlightenment, Jews had intermittently been invited to become part of civil society. But their admittance to it was halfhearted. They didn't have the same rights and privileges as the rest of the population. What attracted Ben-Yehuda to Zionism was the concept of universalism. He wanted to stop seeing Jewish history as an appendix, an exception in world history. *Normality* was the key term. He became convinced that he needed to apply his energy to the quest for Jewish self-determination. But Ben-Yehuda's decision to devote himself to Zionism brought along with it unwelcome consequences. "The rumor passed among my friends that I had become a heretic and was now a different person. Some of them left me," he writes.

A person's life is often decided in a single instant: the instant in which one knows forever who he or she is destined to be. For Ben-Yehuda, the epiphany came in his adolescence, still in Plotzk, when a Talmudic exegete, Rabbi Yossi Bloicker, made him realize that Hebrew was more than the language rabbis had been speaking for generations. Bloicker gave him a copy of *Tzohar ha-Tevah* (*Painter of Nature*), a book of grammar. It revealed to Ben-Yehuda that there were books written in a beautiful style in the sacred tongue. Then Bloicker brought out another book from under the chair, where it had been hidden, and asked Ben-Yehuda to read its title and first paragraph aloud. It was the Hebrew translation from the German by I. Rumsch of *The Adventures of Robinson Crusoe*, published in Vilna in 1861.

Ben-Yehuda was flabbergasted. Could the sacred language, the language of the Bible, the Mishnah, and the Gemara, be used for such mundane matters? Was it possible that the language of King David and the prophets, the language that Maimonides and others had connected with the divine, could convey secular content? No sooner had Ben-Yehuda begun to enjoy *Robinson Crusoe* than someone knocked at the door. Rabbi Bloicker, afraid Defoe's book would be seen by the wrong eyes, grabbed the volume from his pupil's hands and returned it to its secret hiding place. The item was dangerous; it needed to be protected from unwelcome exposure. Ben-Yehuda understood then what Hebrew was capable of. But he also recognized that the road he was about to travel was filled with obstacles.

The serendipity of his encounter with *Robinson Crusoe* allows for another interpretation. Daniel Defoe's novel is a remarkable Hebraist parable—doing it all yourself, making it all by yourself. Maybe Ben-Yehuda himself ought to be seen as Robinson Crusoe, alone on his island, battling the elements, improvising as he goes along, indomitable in his self-reliant spirit.

In a copy of the Russian journal *Vestnik*, Ben-Yehuda read about a character in George Eliot's novel *Daniel Deronda* who promulgated Hebrew as the national language of the Jewish people. Then, around 1877 or 1878, as Russia went to war against Turkey in order to liberate Bulgaria from Turkish rule, he became impressed by the Bulgarian struggle for independence. He wasn't yet twenty years old. A fever of nationalism was spreading across Europe. But Ben-Yehuda's views were already marked by Zionism. If the Bulgarians required their own country, shouldn't Jews embrace a similar dream? For a moment he wondered if Yiddish, not Hebrew, should be the Jewish national language. But he discarded the *mame-loshn* as ungrounded. It was used by the Ashkenazim, the Jews from Eastern Europe, but it didn't connect them to their biblical past. Hebrew did. And so Ben-Yehuda came up with his romantic mission.

The Jewish population worldwide at the end of the nineteenth century was estimated to be 10,600,000. About two-thirds were Yiddish speakers. Russia had a Jewish population of almost 4 million. The United States, where Yiddish was also prominent, had more than a million and a half. Turkey, still the center of the Ottoman Empire, where French, Arabic, and Ladino were spoken, had approximately 282,200 Jews. What kind of plan did Ben-Yehuda have? How would he be able to implement it when a large number of Jews lived in rural areas and were almost illiterate?

In 1879 Ben-Yehuda wrote "The Burning Question," the essay Sáenz-Badillos had discussed with me in his office and arguably Ben-Yehuda's most recognized piece of writing. In it he encourages the embrace of Hebrew as a crucial component of Zionism. In his view, the revival of Jewish nationalism and the resurrection of the biblical tongue went hand in hand: "Let us revive the nation and its tongue will be revived, too!" Historians of the State of Israel see his essay, and the series of letters he wrote to contend with its reception, as a milestone in the history of Zionism. When Ben-Yehuda tried to get "The Burning Question" published, it was swiftly rejected by many magazines. It wasn't until he mailed it to *Ha-Shahar* (*The Dawn*), a periodical edited between 1868 and 1885 by another Lithuanian, Peretz Smolenskin, that the message fell on attentive ears. Smolenskin published "The Burning Question," but with his own rebuttal.

The essay was read widely and generated much controversy among Jewish thinkers. It started an epistolary debate between Ben-Yehuda and Smolenskin. In one letter from 1880, Ben-Yehuda summarizes their back-and-forth:

> Were I not a believer in the redemption of the Jewish people, I would have discarded Hebrew as a useless impediment. I would then agree that the *Maskilim* of Berlin were right in saying that the Hebrew language has purpose only as a bridge to enlightenment. Having despaired of redemption, they could see no other use for this language. For—permit me, sir, to ask you— what is the Hebrew language to a man who is no more a Hebrew [Ben Yehuda's synonym for Jew]? Is it more to him than Latin or Greek? Why should he learn the Hebrew language or read its renascent literature? Why,

indeed, must the "Science of Judaism" be expressed only in Hebrew? Of what value, in fact, is such a science? How can a science which can be discussed only in its original language be worthy of being called knowledge? Where is there a people whose learning and wisdom can be expressed only in its own language?

Elsewhere he adds:

It is plain for all to see, sir, that our youth is abandoning our language—but why? Because in their eyes it is a dead and useless tongue. . . . Only a Hebrew with a Hebrew heart will understand this, and such a man will understand even without our urging. Let us therefore make the language really live again! Let us teach our young to speak it and then they will never betray it!

But we will be able to revive the Hebrew tongue only in a country in which the number of Hebrew inhabitants exceeds the number of gentiles. Therefore, let us increase the number of Jews in our desolate land [Palestine]; let the remnant of our people return to the land of their fathers; *let us revive the nation and its tongue will be revived, too!*

And he concludes:

I therefore contend, sir, that we have strayed from the right path. It is senseless to cry out: Let us cherish the Hebrew language, lest we perish! The Hebrew language can live only if we revive the nation and return it to its fatherland. In the last analysis, this is the only way to achieve our lasting redemption; short of such a solution, we are lost, lost forever! Do you, sir, think otherwise? The Jewish religion will, no doubt, be able to endure even in alien lands; it will adjust its forms to the spirit of the place and the age, and its destiny will parallel that of all religions! But the nation? The nation cannot live except on its own soil; only on this soil can it revive and bear magnificent fruit, as in days of old!

Ben-Yehuda's Zionism was linguistic. You might almost say he wanted Jews to create their own country so that they could speak Hebrew in it. The land was a stepping-stone for linguistic redemption—a way of moving into the future and back to Sinai at the same time.

ה

How to make the dream come true?

At the age of twenty-two, Ben-Yehuda found his mission inchoate. It would take him two decades to sort out the question. Jack Fellman, an American who studied linguistics, semantics, and Middle Eastern studies at Harvard— where he wrote his doctoral dissertation on Ben-Yehuda— summarized Ben-Yehuda's threefold approach: he called the first stage "Hebrew in the Home," the second "Hebrew in the School," and the third "Words, Words, Words."

The first stage required personal sacrifice. Life in Lithuania, Russia, and France (Ben-Yehuda studied at the Sorbonne in Paris) was unacceptable. Ben-Yehuda was ready to make aliyah, to ascend to *Eretz Yisrael.* In 1881, he and his wife, Dvora, moved to Jerusalem via Turkey. The misery and anti-Semitism in the Pale of Settlement at the time had begun to drive Russian Jews to America, where the liberal, educated Ashkenazic Jews from Germany had already put down roots. But the couple moved in the other direction. They arrived in Palestine just as the first wave of settlers were making their way to the *yishuv,* as the early Jewish settlement was then known. That group was called the First Aliyah. Its advent took place between 1882 and 1903. "From the moment my feet trod on the land of my fathers," writes Ben-Yehuda, "I tried with all my might to become a native part of it. I embraced its dust with affection, breathed in its air thirstily, and gazed in delight at its mountains and valleys, at the glorious changes in the colors of its skies, at the rising and setting of its sun. I listened with a feeling of sanctity to the murmurs of its rivers and streams, and I can say that I feel myself to belong altogether to this land, to be a Jerusalemite. I have severed every link between myself and other countries, and I feel love for one land only, the Land of Israel. I love not only the country itself but also its very hardships, its ailments, and its fevers."

It was upon arriving in the Holy Land that Ben-Yehuda Hebraized his name. He felt that Perelman denoted a servile, Diasporic, and hence vilified identity. He wanted to have a new self, a new identity—like Malcolm Little becoming

Malcolm X. In the Torah the father's name established a man's lineage. His father's name had been Yehuda; thus, he chose Ben-Yehuda (son of Yehuda). In addition, Yehuda was the tribe from which modern Jews purportedly descended. By calling himself Eliezer Ben-Yehuda, he would stress his connection with the biblical past.

But the perception of Ben-Yehuda as the sole mover and shaker, the man who redeemed ancient Hebrew and made it into a modern tongue, is false. It was unquestionably a collective effort by a quixotic generation of Zionists who understood the deep connection that existed between language and nationalism. Along with other Zionist teachers, artists, intellectuals, and activists, Ben-Yehuda pushed for the formation of elementary schools and centers of advanced learning, where Hebrew would become a conduit for research in the humanities and the sciences. As time went by, he and others would focus their effort on making Jerusalem the capital of the emerging new culture, in spite of the fact that the city was occupied and that Jaffa was for a while a more suitable place, since it was the thriving port of entry through which the new immigrants passed as they arrived in Palestine.

Ben-Yehuda became involved in editing and writing for the weekly magazine *Ha-Havatzelet* (the word refers to a desert flower), which at the time was under the direction of Israel Dov Frumkin. The connection with Frumkin would lead Ben-Yehuda to start his own publication, a monthly supplement called *Mevasseret Tziyyon* (*The Zion News*). Spreading the gospel through the printed media was crucial. His es-

says, reviews, and columns were invariably about the relevance of Hebrew to the Zionist project. His most important
editing job was in yet another newspaper, the subscription-
based *Ha-Tzvi* (*The Deer*), modeled after *Le Figaro*, in which
he focused far more on lexicographic topics. It was essential
for Ben-Yehuda to bridge the private and public realms. In
his view, the first order of business was to lead a model existence by making Hebrew the family's domestic tongue.

It's difficult to fathom how complicated that decision was.
The sacred tongue, unused for centuries on a daily basis, was
cumbersome. Its archaic lexicon had been frozen since the
Rabbinic period. The language had been spoken in the Tannaitic era (around 200 C.E.), but it gradually evolved into a
literary medium in which the Mishnah, the Tosefta, and the
Tannaitic exegetical commentaries (known as midrashim)
would be written. To make it come alive, Ben-Yehuda would
need to create a bank of modern terms. What would a steam
engine be called? Or a vaccination against polio? Or a street-
light? Hence, the stage of Hebrew in the home entailed verbal improvisation. This is how Ben-Yehuda portrays the
effort in *A Dream Come True:*

> [My first wife] is the first Jewish mother in our time to
> speak to her children in Hebrew from the moment of
> their birth. . . . Our material position was not then one
> of the best. My salary at the Alliance school was, as I
> have already said, fifty francs—which is ten dollars—
> per month, and the remuneration for editing *Havatzelet*
> was twenty francs, which is four dollars, likewise per

month. But these four dollars a month were not paid exactly on time by the publisher of *Havatzelet*. Not, heaven forbid, because of ill will, but simply because he himself did not have them to give me each and every month. With this generous income of about sixty francs, or twelve dollars, a month, it was difficult even at that time in Jerusalem to employ many servants. However, it was possible, even with this income, to keep one maidservant, at least a young one, to perform at least the simpler domestic duties, for at that time one could find a girl of about fifteen to serve a house for half a *mejida* a month, which is less than a half-dollar.

The excerpt offers a glimpse of *yishuv* life—with servants and all. It surely challenges the common belief that all settlers were equally destitute. He continues:

And the pregnant woman, the future mother of the boy, was weak and frail by nature, and her stressful life, the pregnancy, and then the birth weakened her even more. Nevertheless, she agreed willingly not to employ a housemaid, so that the child would not hear the sounds of any language other than Hebrew. We were afraid the walls of the house, the very air in our room, would absorb the sounds of the foreign language as they issued from the mouth of the maidservant, and their echo would reach the ears of the child. We feared that those foreign sounds would impair his faculty for hearing Hebrew, the Hebrew words would not be absorbed adequately and properly, and the child might not speak Hebrew. Experience proved afterwards that these were superfluous, exaggerated fears. We saw many examples afterwards in which children who grew up in an environment that was not purely Hebrew, and whose ears were not as protected against the absorption of non-Hebrew sounds, nevertheless grew up speaking Hebrew as long as the main language in the home was Hebrew and the father and mother spoke Hebrew. Moreover, subsequent experience also proved that in a Hebrew home, where people spoke only Hebrew to one another and were punctilious in their Hebrew speech, the maidservant herself, especially if she was young, quickly learned the words that were for everyday domestic life and was herself careful to avoid uttering foreign words. All this we learnt from later experience, when Hebrew speech among children was already a fact and there was no place for doubt about its feasibility.

Ben-Yehuda is unconsciously portraying himself as Robinson Crusoe. But there are also biblical echoes in the passage: Palestine is presented as a Garden of Eden, Dvora is Eve, and Hebrew is a mechanism transforming religious values into linguistic redemption. To succeed in their pursuit, the couple needed to get all the inner strength they could muster and face a degrading environment:

But at the beginning of the experiment, when everything was still in doubt, we feared even the remotest eventuality. We wanted to surround the child's speech with one protective fence after another, one wall after another, in order to keep away from his ears any admixture of foreign sounds. This holy soul, who was destined to be the first mother in the era of national revival, who was to supply the nation with a generation of Hebrew speakers, willingly took upon herself the hardships of raising a child without the most elementary domestic help, even though she was herself very weak and frail. The dear soul stood this hard test for a long time, alone and unaided doing all the domestic chores, and also all the work of caring for the child—until the danger passed, until it was granted to us to hear the first stammering of Hebrew words coming out of the child's mouth, until it was granted to us to hear childish babble in Hebrew.

One of Ben-Yehuda's early goals (the second stage in his plan for linguistic resurrection) was to make Hebrew the language of instruction in Jewish schools all over Palestine. This task also proved challenging. He got a job as a teacher in schools managed by the Alliance Israélite Universelle, an international organization founded in Paris in 1860, which was created to improve on the education and professional development of Jews around the world but also committed to the principle of self-sufficiency. In Palestine at the time, the pedagogical models were European. Hebrew had never been a language taught in secular classrooms. There weren't any textbooks available. Along with his teaching colleagues, Ben-Yehuda was forced to improvise.

Other teachers have left testimonies of the task. One of them, David Yellin, a friend and supporter of Ben-Yehuda, stated: "Every teacher had a French or Russian teaching book of his own, and he organized his Hebrew work according to it. . . . Terms for teaching did not exist. Every village teacher was an Academy [of the Hebrew Language] member with respect to creating words according to his taste, and everyone, of course, used his own creations." Similarly, David Yudeleviz, another teacher, commented: "Without books, expressions, words, verbs and hundreds of nouns, we had to begin teaching. It is impossible to describe or imagine under what pressure the first seeds were planted. . . . Hebrew teaching materials for elementary education were limited. We were half-mute, stuttering, we spoke with our hands and eyes." The penury, in Ben-Yehuda's opinion, was worth it. In 1886, he wrote in *Ha-Tzvi:* "The Hebrew language will go from the synagogue to the house of study, and from the house of study to the school, and from the school it will come into the home and . . . become a living language."

Orthodox communities had lived in Palestine for centuries. The magnetism of the Holy Land kept the place alive. But those Jews were few in number. They lived in precarious economic conditions, mostly sustained by the *halukkah* system, an organized collection of money designed to support Jews about to make aliyah and poor Jews already living in Palestine. Initially Ben-Yehuda thought he could convince the Orthodox to share his dream. It was a foolish thought. In her biography, Dvorah Omer talks about how immigrants applauded Ben-Yehuda, but the rabbis despised him. They "regarded him as an infidel for daring to use the holy tongue for everyday matters." Their objection targeted both his teaching and his ideas. He had become active in politics, asking people to support Zionism without reservation. "They objected violently to the articles in his papers which advocated the return of Jews to farming and labor. They instructed their followers not to subscribe to the paper."

But the situation was more complex. Joseph Gedaliah Klausner, another influential Zionist and a celebrated scholar of Jewish religion, history, and literature who also made aliyah from Lithuania, once remarked on this captivating aspect of Ben-Yehuda's personality: his impostorship. Klausner stated that when Ben-Yehuda and Dvora arrived in Jerusalem, so as "to ingratiate himself with the Orthodox Jews who knew written Hebrew and could, therefore, readily speak the language, Ben-Yehuda at first adopted their customs." To achieve his objective, Ben-Yehuda returned to the ways of his childhood, which he had repudiated as a student of the gymnasium. "He grew a beard and earlocks, and prevailed upon his wife to wear a *sheytl* [wig]." But, according to Klausner, the strategy backfired. "The Orthodox Jews of Jerusalem soon sensed that for Ben-Yehuda Hebrew was not a holy tongue, but a secular, national tongue, and that his purpose for introducing spoken Hebrew was solely nationalist and political. They began to suspect him, and Ben-Yehuda became an extremist in his antireligious attitude. He registered as a national Jew 'without religion.' " That opposition from the Orthodox would color his entire career; actually, it would outlast him. To this day there are segments of the ultra-Orthodox world that see him as the enemy. They are appalled by his dishonesty. Did he really pretend to be one of them in order to advance his mission?

There was suspicion enough that when Ben-Yehuda's wife died in 1891, he was told she wasn't a believer and would thus need to be laid to rest outside the confines of a Jewish cemetery. He was furious. The dispute was eventually resolved, but it left a wound in him that would be reopened years later. By then he had married Dvora's sister, Hemda. This practice was not uncommon at the time. On her deathbed, Dvora herself made the arrangement: "If you want to be a queen," she wrote her sister, "hurry to Jerusalem and marry my prince, my darling Eliezer." As it turned out, for decades Hemda would fight at Ben-Yehuda's side to achieve the dream of reviving Hebrew, to the point not only of producing stories, translations, manifestos, newspaper columns, and even a biography (or better, a hagiography, for Ben-Yehuda was a saint in her eyes), but also of contributing to his dictionary (among others, she coined the word *ofnah*, fashion) and traveling to Europe in search of a publisher and funds for the enterprise.

Eventually, the Orthodox, in cahoots with the Ottoman rulers, increased the pressure on Ben-Yehuda to an extreme. They found an article that his mentor, Samuel Naphtali Herz Jonas, had written in 1894 for a Hanukkah issue of *Ha-Tzvi* that included the phrase "let us gather strength and go forward." As Joseph Klausner later attested, "Some of Ben-Yehuda's more bigoted enemies distorted its meaning and interpreted it to the Turkish authorities as 'let us gather an army and proceed against the East.' [He] was charged with sedition." While the Turkish authorities held him, the affair became news around the Jewish world. Furthermore, just as they had done to Baruch Spinoza and other heretics in the past, the Jewish religious authorities in Turkey—in partnership with their Orthodox colleagues in Jerusalem—pronounced a *herem*, a ban that excommunicated him. In *Tongue of the Prophets*, one of the Ben-Yehuda biographies, its author, Robert St. John, an Associated Press reporter, describes the trial that ensued. News items were published regularly in Istanbul, Vilna, Odessa, Paris, London, and New York. "Finally it came down to a cable from ben Yehuda [to his family] which contained just one Hebrew word: *zakkay*, innocent," stated St. John. A one-year prison sentence was handed down, but he was allowed to post bail. More important, he could appeal the sentence. What he couldn't do, according to the Ottoman rule, was continue publishing *Ha-Tzvi*. And he needed to curtail his educational activities.

It was time for Ben-Yehuda to refocus his life. His passion was lexicography. He wanted to justify his life by creating a dictionary that would rehabilitate the sacred tongue, making it usable in Palestine for the thousands of Jewish settlers. After the affair with the Orthodox, he didn't want to think about anything else.

א

I was taken by Ben-Yehuda's tribulations: he had betrayed the Orthodox, whose traditions had inspired him; he was excommunicated from his own people; he turned to a dictionary the way Rashi turned to commentary; and he found newness in an old language and was unswerving through its inversions, transmutations, and reconfigurations.

My explorations of Ben-Yehuda's journey had thus far been secondhand. I needed to experience the impact of his revival, to be a witness.

I decided to share my dream with several Israeli friends. I e-mailed Hillel Halkin, an American-born author, journalist, and translator who lives in Zikhron Ya'akov. Halkin has rendered into English the work of S. Y. Agnon and A. B. Yehoshua, among his many translations, but in my view his best aren't from the Hebrew but from the Yiddish. His versions of Sholem Aleichem's *Tevye the Dairyman* and *The Railroad Stories* are simply superb. A fervent Zionist, Halkin is a surprisingly romantic essayist of strong views. On a couple of occasions (for example, in a piece in *Commentary*) he has written about "the language wars" between Hebrew and Yiddish, attacked Jewish settlers for stealing Arab olives, and denounced the complacency of American Jews who refuse to understand that the logic of their own Jewish commitment demands that they ask themselves seriously why they aren't living in Israel. Halkin believes that "the idea of a Palestinian State alongside Israel in the West Bank and Gaza Strip is not one that I contemplate with particular pleasure . . . and I fear that in relinquishing any part of Palestine I must relinquish a part of myself." Yet he supports the relinquishing of most, though not all, of Judea, Samaria, and Gaza on the premise that it is good for Israel, and because he trusts that the Palestinians, like the Jews, should have a right to create their own state, regardless of what they end up doing with that right.

Halkin agreed to join me in a series of conversations as we drove around Israel.

I also communicated with Eliezer Nowodworski (yes, another Eliezer), a translator and interpreter by trade who makes his home in Tel Aviv. For the last couple of years, Nowodworski and I had corresponded online. In one of my e-mails I had said I was curious about Ben-Yehuda's status as an early Zionist and about the intersection of ideology and language in modern Israel. Did Israelis today still feel close to Ben-Yehuda's mission? Was there a museum dedicated to him somewhere? I asked Nowodworski if he, too, would be willing to wander the country with me, talking to teachers, waitresses, taxi drivers, academics, politicos, soldiers, and prostitutes about Ben-Yehuda and his legacy.

An Argentine Jew who made aliyah in the early seventies, Nowodworski is charming and all-encompassing in his knowledge. Slightly younger than I am, he awakens in me a strange reaction whenever we are together: I see him as my doppelgänger, the uncowardly me who didn't give up on Israel as such, but instead stayed around to fight the fight.

The day he greeted me at Ben-Gurion Airport, Nowodworski was wearing a T-shirt and worn-out jeans, and large bifocals. "Do you know that not since the Babylonian exile in 586 B.C.E. have all Jews used a single language?" he asked.

Nowodworski is a grandson of Shmuel Rollansky, a Warsaw intellectual who became a founding figure of the Jewish community in Buenos Aires (the *yishuv*, as he called it). Rollansky promoted Yiddish in South America through institutions like the YIVO and the Isaac Leib Peretz school in Argentina (Rollansky believed that had Peretz—one of the three "greats of Yiddish literature"—lived longer, he would have immigrated to Argentina). Rollansky championed special culture festivals, wrote a regular column called *"Shtrijn"* ("Features") for *Di Idishe Tzaitung* (*The Yiddish Daily*), was a theater lover, a teacher of teachers, and, perhaps most important, at least for me, the publisher of a set of one hundred volumes of *Musterwerk fun der Idisher Literatur* (*Masterworks of Yiddish Literature*), an anthology attempting to include just about every literary manifestation in Yiddish from anywhere around the globe.

In Toronto, at a translators' conference, Nowodworski and I had discussed at length the revival of Hebrew and the connection between language and cultural identity. I remember arguing that these two categories cannot exist in isolation: a group defined by its own specificity needs a tongue to define its character, and vice versa; a language without a particular group of speakers to support it is impossible to imagine. The United States, for example, defines its own collective identity based on preestablished geographical borders, a mission and a shared sense of history, a flag and an anthem, and English, the primary language of communication among its citizens. There are other tongues spoken in the country, immigrant tongues for the most part. Yet English is the equalizer, the grinding device through which every experience, private and public, is processed to become American. As if to prove my point, I showed Nowodworski a quote I found in *Journal of a Tour to the Hebrides*, James Boswell's travelogue, published in 1785, describing his trip with Samuel Johnson, the great eighteenth-century lexicographer and man of letters. " 'Alas! Sir, what can a nation that has not letters tell of its origin?' " Elsewhere, Dr. Johnson added: "A thousand, nay, a million of children could not invent a language. . . . Inspiration seems to me to be necessary to give man the faculty of speech; to inform him that he may have speech; which I think he could no more find out without inspiration than cows or hogs could think of such a faculty."

The conversation moved to the subject of alphabets. Nowodworski explained that at least on the surface, a language is nothing but the rearrangement—deliberate at first sight, arbitrary when seen sub specie aeternitatis—of letters. "The word *alphabet* comes from the Latin *alphabētum* and the Greek *alpha* and *bēta*," he said. "An alphabet is a phonetic writing system made of symbols representing individual vowel and consonant sounds. Each of these symbols, also known as *letter* (a word with an obscure etymological origin, whose foundation is probably the Latin *littera* that replaced the Greek *grámma*), represents the basic sounds of a language. The same alphabet might be used by more than one nation, but a language is more unique." Nowodworski stressed, however, that not all languages are letter-based. "Some, like Mandarin, are pictographic."

He added that the transition to an alphabetic system, based on phonemes and on symbols representing those phonemes, took place over hundreds of years. "It started in approximately 1700 B.C.E.," he said. "There are dozens of alphabets in use nowadays, the majority of them linear. In Mandarin and Korean, the pictograph still coexists as a system. As various alphabets evolved, they moved in different directions. There are some that use symbols to represent vowels and consonants, such as Latin, English, French, and Portuguese. Others are known as consonantaries, using one symbol per consonant, as in the case of Hebrew, Aramaic, Arabic, and Persian. And there are languages described as syllabaries, in which syllables make up words, for instance Cherokee, the African language Vai, and the Chinese language Yi. These three approaches are sometimes combined. And a combination of alphabet and pictogram is still used, and is probably increasing with globalization. The signs in an airport for toilets and telephones or the icons in computer software are proof."

Then Nowodworski threw me a sinker ball: "How many languages are there altogether, Ilan?"

I had read somewhere that there are approximately seven thousand different languages in use in the world today.

"And how many of them use an alphabet?"

I guessed a small fraction.

He continued: "And how many more have disappeared over time?"

I didn't know the answer.

"Probably twice that amount: twelve thousand," said Nowodworski. "It is said that an endangered language disappears every two weeks. It does so in an instant, as the last speaker dies."

He asked if I knew what percentage had been adopted as a "national" language. I didn't want to venture an uneducated guess. "The answer depends on what one understands by the concept of nation," he said. "Take Latin America. There are twenty different independent nations, two French protectorates, two Dutch dependencies, and two more U.S. dependencies (Puerto Rico and the Virgin Islands). But several of those twenty are only nations in name. Internal communication between provinces is sometimes difficult. The central government doesn't have jurisdiction over the entire population. In some cases, there isn't a single language in the entire territory. Guarani, Quechua, Aymara, Mixtec, and other aboriginal tongues are still in use. There are also foreign tongues employed by small bastions of people, such as Welsh and Cantonese."

My dialogue with Nowodworski made me see Hebrew simultaneously as Israel's official tongue and as an ethnic, religious, and transnational vehicle of communication used by Jews worldwide. More than anything, I began to think of it as a state of mind. Yehuda Halevi, in *Kitab al Khazari*, originally written in Arabic in the first half of the twelfth century and rendered in Hebrew by the legendary translator Judah ibn Tibbon, suggested that "Israel amidst the nations is like the heart amidst the organs of the body, at once the most sick and most healthy of them." This is definitely true with language. Germany uses German, France French, Italy Italian. But Hebrew, having been an imperial language at the time of King David, became stateless after the destruction of the Second Temple by the Romans in 70 C.E. It was no longer attached to a single piece of land. It became an itinerant tongue. And its alphabet fostered the formation of numerous tongues used by the Jews at various stages, including Aramaic, Ladino, and Yiddish. In Dr. Johnson's wise appreciation, Hebrew letters don't point exclusively to the formation of the State of Israel. Their history is more global.

And more complex. The richness of the Hebrew language

is connected with its transnational evolution. This might sound like an anachronism to some, for Hebrew is the Holy Tongue, divinely inspired, a gift from heaven.

When I arrived in Tel Aviv, Nowodworski greeted me warmly in three languages: Spanish, Yiddish, and Hebrew. Next he asked if I wanted to rent a cell phone; a store at the airport specializes in cell phone rentals. "It's almost impossible to travel in *Eretz Yisrael* without your gadget," Nowodworski announced.

I found it emblematic that, on a trip devoted to an ancestral language, my first conversation was about using a technological device for my voice to travel through a satellite.

"In the United States I'm bombarded with calls to my cell phone," I answered. "If possible, I'd like to take a break, resorting when needed to the old-fashioned public phones."

"An endangered species," Nowodworski said. "Israelis are constantly in contact with each other. It's part of our besieged mentality."

He was the guide I wanted, my Virgil. Were Israelis proud of Hebrew? How did the language they employ today connect with their past? Did they still see Hebrew through the prism of the Zionist dream that led to the creation of the Jewish State in 1948? In what sense had Hebrew matured in the last decades? What kind of connection did the Hebrew language have with other tongues, like Arabic, English, and Russian?

"You won't have a shortage of schmooze, *querido*," Nowodworski said to me as we walked out of Ben-Gurion and into the street in search of a taxi. "But you'll have to abide by the contradictions that emerge before your ears. Jews in general, and Israelis in particular, are notorious for offering conflicting views."

The taxi dropped us at my hotel. I checked into my room, shaved, and freshened myself a bit.

Half an hour later we were walking on the streets of downtown Tel Aviv. It was late on a breezy Saturday afternoon, the end of the weekend for Israelis. The Orthodox community was still at prayer and the streets were almost empty. Children were playing in the park. Dog walkers were patiently making their way across boulevards, stopping to greet a neighbor, evading a fast Rollerblader, picking up after their pets. Swimmers were returning from the beach.

Nowodworski pointed forward with his right hand. "You see that street?"

I nodded.

"It's Ben-Yehuda Street. Almost every major city in Israel has a street named after him. This one runs parallel to the Mediterranean coastline. A block from here, it intersects with Ben-Gurion Street. But if I'm not mistaken, the two patriarchs never came that close. Ben-Yehuda died in 1922. He was ostracized in Zionist circles, perceived as a lunatic. The *yishuv* was a small place in the early decades of the twentieth century. Still, Ben-Gurion, the George Washington of Israel, never met him. Issues of language were important to the first prime minister, but never as important as spreading the gospel of political Zionism."

"Is there a worse form of immortality than ending up as a street name?" I asked. "As you know, in Mexico this might be the way for the establishment to deprive someone of a legacy: force people to remember your name, but not what you did."

Nowodworski laughed. "Cecil Roth once said that before Ben-Yehuda, Jews *could* speak Hebrew, but after him they *did*. It isn't totally true, though."

"Why?"

"It's a known secret that he didn't revive Hebrew."

"What did he do, then?"

"Well, he convinced himself he did. But others were equally involved in the endeavor. I would say that rather than praising him for reviving a moribund tongue, we should credit Ben-Yehuda for reinventing it." Nowodworski took a breath. "Keep in mind that the second half of the nineteenth century was a time of linguistic utopias. Take the case of Esperanto, an international language created by a doctor, Ludwik Lazar Zamenhof, born in Bialystok, then in Russian-ruled Poland, in 1859 (a year after Ben-Yehuda) to parents of Lithuanian Jewish descent. A Zionist who was nominated for the Nobel Peace Prize in 1910 but failed to get it, Zamenhof died in Warsaw in 1917 and is buried in the Okopowa Street Jewish Cemetery. The vocabulary of Esperanto is derived from the Romance, Germanic, and Slavic languages, although the logic of Esperanto is derived from the use in Hebrew of consonant stems. For instance, in Esperanto the word *sano*, meaning 'health,' is related to the words *sana*, 'healthy,' *sanulo*, 'a healthy person,' *sanilo*, 'a cure, medicine,' *sane*, 'healthily,' *malsano*, 'illness,' *sanigi*, 'to cure,' and *malsanulejo*, 'hospital.' It's the exact same structure!"

I was surprised not to be exhausted after a fourteen-hour

flight. On the contrary, I was exuberant. The conversation was putting my mind to work.

Soon Nowodworski and I were walking on Ibn Gabirol Street, between the Tel Aviv City Hall and Gan Ha'ir, near the memorial stone that marks the site where Yitzhak Rabin was assassinated.

Pointing at it, Nowodworski said: "They come and go. Our political leaders manipulate us. They look for ways to implement their own dreams. Some die in the process." We were now looking at the memorial. An adjacent wall still displayed the graffiti painted by young Israelis lamenting Rabin's departure and the death of a peace process. "Only their language remains," said Nowodworski.

As we walked toward my hotel, he commented: "I'm not sure how many young Israelis today are able to recognize, with precision, the fathers of Zionism. But there's a song about Ben-Yehuda. Do you know it?"

He was referring to a ballad composed by Yaron London with music by the popular baritone singer Matti Caspi. The ballad was made famous by Chava Alberstein on her album *Songs of My Beloved Country.* This English translation is by Malka Tischler:

Like the prophets, zealous about *Hashem,*
he was zealous about the verb, the adjective, and the
    noun.
And at midnight, oil lamp in his window,
he would write in his dictionary stacks
and stacks of pretty words, words
which fly, which roll from the tongue.

Eliezer, when will you lie down to sleep?
You're practically bent over.
And Hebrew, which has waited two thousand years,
will still be waiting for you at dawn.

Eliezer Ben-Yehuda,
an amusing Jew.
Words, words, words
he invented with his feverish brain.

As Nowodworski recited the lyrics, I realized that this
was the only song I knew about a lexicographer. It plays on
words, as in *Hashem*, meaning God (literally, the Name), and
shem, which also means "noun," as in the second line of the
first stanza above. It also plays on Ben-Yehuda's obsession
with words, definitions, the biblical past, and his own legacy
as a founding father of Zionism. As Tischler suggested in
a note accompanying her translation, it pays attention to
biographical facts, such as that Ben-Yehuda suffered from
tuberculosis and worked standing up, so as not to give in to
tiredness. Even if he wasn't solely responsible for the revival
of Hebrew, the song stresses Ben-Yehuda's symbolic status
as torchbearer:

If Hebrew has slept for two thousand years, *nu*, so
    what?
Come, let's wake it up, and invent initiative
    [*yotzmah*],
clothes iron [*mag-hetz*], bomb [*p'tzatzah*],
furniture [*rihut*].

With feather tip, in fluid writing,
he wrote cauliflower [*k'ruvit*], he wrote ice cream
   [*g'lidah*];
he wrote all of the Ben-Yehuda dictionary.
And he went on creating words,
and his fast quill didn't rest,
and the language grew
and didn't recognize itself in the morning.

   Eliezer Ben-Yehuda . . .

And when a son was born to him, he said:
This firstborn I will call Ben-Yehuda, Itamar,
   who from infancy to withering,
from the day of his entering the covenant
   [*brit-milah*] until his death,
will have a covenant with Hebrew,
and will fight to wipe out foreign languages.
Itamar truly became a man,
tall, handsome, and well-spoken,
and the language he spoke was Hebrew.
Itamar Ben-Avi,
whose father was a prophet,
a man after my own heart.

   Eliezer Ben-Yehuda . . .

"Itamar Ben-Avi was Ben-Yehuda's eldest son," I said to
Nowodworski, proud of my knowledge. "One of a total of

eleven siblings. Ben-Yehuda raised him in linguistic isolation—not even allowing the child, as he wrote, 'to hear the
songs of birds'—so that he would be 'the first Hebrew-
speaking child.' "

Nowodworski told me, "Ben-Avi became one of the most
distinguished Hebrew-language journalists of his generation." Although the song makes reference to the *brit milah*,
the circumcision covenant between a Jewish boy and God, in
Ben-Yehuda's antireligious mind, his son's covenant was first
and foremost with Hebrew.

As an experiment to find out if Israelis know about Ben-
Yehuda, I stopped at a corner newsstand, where I bought
copies of Friday's weekend editions of *Haaretz* and *Maariv*,
Israel's major dailies. After receiving my change, I asked the
shop clerk if she knew who Ben-Yehuda was. She was an artificial blonde, wearing an Adidas tracksuit that emphasized
her hips and protruding belly. Her initial response was a
smile, followed by a silence, behind which I detected hesita-
tion. "Ben-Yehuda? It's a street," she replied.

"But who is it named after?"

"How should I know? Am I an encyclopedia?"

↑

It took me no time to recognize that at the dawn of the
twenty-first century, Israel was a sum of divergent selves. A
thriving democracy, it was filled with McDonald's, shopping
malls, Internet cafés, and an abundance of other capitalist

symbols. Just like the United States, it was decadent in its embrace of leisure. In the hotel where I stayed, I saw a masseuse (I assume she was a prostitute) wearing a tank top with the American flag on it, one of its fifty stars replaced by a Star of David.

Nowodworski had told me that there are approximately eight million Hebrew speakers in the world today. Three-fourths of them are in Israel. The number would have made Ben-Yehuda proud. But in the international hierarchy of tongues it is microscopic. In the year 2000 Mandarin had a billion speakers, English five hundred million, Spanish four hundred million, and Hindi almost three hundred million. And yet, when placed along a trajectory that spans almost three millennia, the surging of Hebrew is nothing short of miraculous, especially when one considers that at the end of the nineteenth century the estimate of Hebrew speakers globally was not even a meager ten thousand.

The question is what kind of Hebrew is being used by its speakers. Like English, Hebrew is to be admired for its current plasticity. Successive waves of immigrants to Israel, Jewish and non-Jewish, have influenced its syntax. The dominance of Ashkenazic culture began to crumble in the fifties with arrivals from the former Ottoman Empire. Ethiopians, whose connection to Hebrew dates back to biblical times, came in the early eighties. The Sephardic accents of descendants of Jews expelled from Spain became essential ingredients. So did Mizrahi accents from what is known as the Levant, the geographical area within the Middle East south of the Taurus Mountains, bounded by the Mediterranean

Sea on the west, the northern Arabian Desert to the south, and the region that once was Upper Mesopotamia and is Iraq today on the east. Then came the collapse of the Soviet Union in 1991. A substantial number of Russian Jews made aliyah, infusing the language with Slavic terms.

In a country constantly defined by war, keeping in touch is a way to feel alive. Everywhere one looks, there are young soldiers. And the sound of ambulances doesn't appear to bother anyone. A rocket might have been thrown from Gaza. Tanks might have been mobilized near the West Bank. A suicide bomber might have been caught near a bus station. It's the pressure of living in a constant state of emergency. People just go about their business pretending everything is normal. And, indeed, this is normality for most of them.

That attitude among Israelis is admirable if unnerving. Literally everyone I spoke with while searching for Ben-Yehuda's past had some proximity to the threat of death: a wounded husband in the Sinai, a deceased daughter in a massacre in Haifa, a depressed friend unwilling to leave his apartment in Rehovot. Maybe this proximity is what gives the Israeli character what a Chicago-born sociologist I spoke to calls "the three r's": rawness, roughness, and rudeness. The realization that no matter what you do, how much you try to follow a routine, terror will come close to you one way or another makes Israelis impatient—not only with the world but with themselves. "Don't forget we're in the middle of the desert," she said. "The animals in the desert aren't known for their gentility. The dry environment has them in a constant state of alertness." She took a breath. "Being an Israeli turns you into a target. No matter where you go, if you're sunbathing, backpacking, or simply applying for a job in a foreign country, you're always aware of it."

While the sociologist talked, I thought to myself that in this way Israelis are similar to the Jews in the Diaspora: they don't want to be confined to four walls, any four walls, no matter where they are. Their metabolism is at once centripetal and centrifugal.

During lunch in a fancy Tel Aviv shopping center, I ordered a leafy salad with multigrain bread and a carrot juice. The waitress who served me had an Iranian accent. She asked me where I had learned my Hebrew. I told her in Mexican schools.

"You mean Jewish schools, don't you?" she wondered.

I laughed. "Who else but Jews would want to speak it?"

She said she had been to Mexico not long ago. I later found out she fit into a pattern of young Israeli military recruits: once they complete their military service, they leave the country for a year. In the early nineties their destination of choice was India, especially Mumbai. Thousands of Israelis lived in ashrams in various provinces. In the late nineties Brazil became all the rage, though people also went to Mexico and some countries in Central America, such as Costa Rica and Ecuador. (They avoided Nicaragua, El Salvador, and Guatemala because of the political strife, and Honduras because it didn't have a tourist infrastructure.)

It isn't shocking to hear Spanish among twentysomething Israelis, an ungrammatical Spanish, impure, spontaneous. As it happens, shortly before, I had stopped at a branch of Steimatzky, a bookstore chain, and browsed through the travel section. There was a plethora of guides, all in Hebrew, for inexpensive trips for a generation eager to escape the pressures of having to defend the country from its enemies every day of the year. Colombia is a destination, but, since a kidnapping of Israelis some years ago, it has been placed on the "to avoid" list. This isn't an exception. On an annual basis, there is an onslaught of tragic news coming from these countries: of Israelis suffering accidents or disappearing in Chile's Araucaria, Argentina's Patagonia, or Bolivia's Andean region. Several cases of AIDS have been connected with these destinations, especially with the Carnival season in Brazil, known for its promiscuity.

There are also positive aspects. In Quito, for instance, Israelis take Spanish-language lessons, which they show off when they return home. A few opt to stay forever, opening restaurants and other businesses. (In Mexico City, there's a Mediterranean restaurant called Falafel Benzona, a play on Hebrew words that, if translated into Spanish, would be the equivalent of Falafel Hijo de Puta, and in English Falafel Son of a Bitch. In Buenos Aires, a bar features the name Dak, a subtle play on *bardak*, the Hebrew word for both a total mess and a brothel.) Mexican, Colombian, and Venezuelan *telenovelas* are extremely popular in Israel. Some experts believe their popularity has to do not only with the melodramatic nature of the material but with the interest in Latin America of a young generation that has spent time there.

The waitress asked me what I did for a living. I told her I was a teacher.

"Of what?"

"Literature," I replied.

Immediately, she recited for me in Hebrew a poem by Yehuda Amichai—here in an English translation by Chana Bloch:

The diameter of the bomb was thirty centimeters
and the diameter of its effective range about seven
    meters,
with four dead and eleven wounded.
And around these, in a large circle
of pain and time, two hospitals are scattered
and one graveyard. But the young woman
who was buried in the city she came from,
at a distance of more than a hundred kilometers,
enlarges the circle considerably,
and the solitary man mourning the death
at the distant shores of a country far across the sea
includes the entire world in the circle.
And I won't even mention the howl of orphans
that reaches up to the throne of God and
beyond, making
a circle with no end and no God.

I was impressed. In how many countries does a waitress recite to you a poem about death? The fact that it was a poem by Amichai made it all the more significant to me because he was born in Würzburg, Germany, two years after Ben-Yehuda's death. He, too, came from a religious background. His family immigrated to Palestine in 1935, when he was eleven, and settled in Jerusalem a year later. Amichai's real name was Ludwig Pfeuffer. Like Ben-Yehuda, he replaced his given name with an invented one as an assertion of national identity. Amichai was among the first to use colloquial Israeli Hebrew in his poetry.

I asked the waitress if she had known him before he died in 2000. "He once came to our elementary school," she replied. "He recited his poems softly, without pretense, making everyone feel they wanted to be near him, to touch him, to fall in love with him."

That evening I went to the fashionable Performing Arts Center in Tel Aviv for a contemporary staging of Shakespeare's *Hamlet* by the Cameri Theater troupe, known for its repertory of socially responsible plays. Directed by Omri Nitzan, the cast plays with rotating chairs and mingles with the audience, making the experience more immediate. Nitzan transported the rottenness in Denmark to an Israel that since the Six-Day War has been run by corrupt political leaders whose hands are covered in blood. I was impressed by the performance, but I was mesmerized and moved by the sheer chance to hear the Bard in Hebrew. The lucid translation was by T. Carmi, from the early eighties, but Carmi was far from the first to bring Shakespeare's play into Hebrew. One of the earliest efforts was by H. Y. Borenstein in Warsaw in 1926, followed by others in 1942 and 1944. For years the canonical translation of Shakespeare was Abraham Shlonsky's, released in Tel Aviv in 1946, although it is a well-known fact that Shlonsky's English was poor and that his translation was made using Russian and German parallel texts. Aside from Carmi's, whose version was a challenge to Shlonsky's hegemony, there's a translation by Aharon Komem and a more modern one by Avi Oz.

Given that Hebrew was officially linked to a national condition only in the middle of the twentieth century, the plethora of Hebrew *Hamlet*s is nothing short of breathtaking. It sometimes seems as if Hebrew translators have been in a race to catch up with other modern languages. How many versions of the play are there in French? Just as many, I guess. And maybe fewer in the same span of time.

There were no professional theaters in Palestine in Ben-Yehuda's time. People were busy building a homeland. Yet it's intriguing to imagine him watching a Shakespeare play —in Hebrew. He would surely have been enthralled. According to lexicographic studies, the Bible has a vocabulary of approximately six thousand different words. Shakespeare uses a bank of around thirty-five thousand. That, in a nutshell, is Ben-Yehuda's dream of making the sacred tongue less constrained, more elastic, a language that could reflect the depth and complexity of life in seventeenth-century London, and of life today.

ח

I went out the next day looking for concrete traces of Eliezer Ben-Yehuda in Israel. My intention was to start with the museum dedicated to him.

There is no such thing, though. Nor are his houses open to visitors. Israel has sites dedicated to Bialik and Agnon. There are items from Ahad Ha-Am's workplace in a special collection at Tel Aviv's public library. But Ben-Yehuda appears to have been forgotten by state and local officials as well as by the academic community.

The closest thing to a Ben-Yehuda memorial is the makeshift re-creation of his office in a basement on one of the campuses of the Hebrew University. It is a single dusty room of about twelve by fifteen feet, dark, without air circulation, sparsely furnished. It contains Ben-Yehuda's desk and chair, along with some poorly framed photographs and drawings of him as well as a picture of his tombstone. No labels allow the visitor to identify the items. If the information in St. John's biography is to be trusted, plenty of items were missing: notebooks, ink, a chaise longue, a wastebasket, and a sign that Ben-Yehuda hung on the wall, which he adapted from the tractate of the Mishnah known as *Pirke Avot:*

The day is long,
the work to be done so great!

The smell of the room made me think of my grandmother's bedroom in her home on Avenida Amsterdam in Mexico City, which I used to visit every Friday night. It was dark and unventilated. An air of oppressiveness permeated the entire place. The office re-creation gave me an impression of Ben-Yehuda as a rigid, unwelcoming man.

Nowodworski was accompanying me that day. A staff person led us into the room. There were some two thousand books shelved on the walls, haphazardly organized. There were titles on history, geography, mathematics, biology, and anatomy, as well as a vast number of lexicons. The staff person said that they constituted Ben-Yehuda's own library, but he wasn't certain if these were all his books or if there had been more that for some reason didn't make it to the basement.

I browsed around. Since there were no restrictions on what could be touched, I opened a few books. I saw titles in Russian, German, Greek, Latin, French, Romanian, Polish, and Italian. I was struck by the absence of Yiddish books. "Why aren't there any titles in *der mame-loshn*?" I asked.

Nowodworski appeared uncomfortable with the question. After a minute or two of looking around, he just shrugged.

To refocus our attention, the staff person showed us a volume used by Ben-Yehuda with marginalia he had written while compiling entries for what would become his most ambitious project, the *Dictionary of the Hebrew Language, Ancient and Modern*. Like Moses, who didn't make it to the Promised Land, Ben-Yehuda didn't finish all the volumes of the project. After his death, his second wife and his son Ehud continued the publication. With a total of seventeen volumes and an introductory book called *Prolegomenon* (in Hebrew, *Ha-Mavo ha-Gadol*), the enterprise was completed in 1959 by Moses Hirsch Segal and Naphtali Herz Tur-Sinai.

"It's the source of much of what we do today in the Academy," the staff person stated.

"Really?" I was curious. "Is Ben-Yehuda watching over your shoulders and those of other staffers?"

He laughed. "No, but he's a kind of *saba*." In Hebrew, the word means "grandfather."

Clearly, I wasn't altogether wrong in thinking of my grandmother's home.

As I wandered around, I thought of another library I had

visited, one far more complete and better preserved, which once had belonged to the lexicographer Antonio de Nebrija. Nebrija is credited with publishing the first grammar of the Spanish language. It came out in 1492, the same year Christopher Columbus embarked on his first journey across the Atlantic Ocean and the Jews were expelled from the Iberian Peninsula by the Catholic monarchs Isabella and Ferdinand. Nebrija had made it his task to legitimize Spanish, a vernacular at the time. Realizing it had a bright future, he described Spanish as "the companion of empire." Although the language of knowledge was Latin, he was in love with *el español*.

During a visit to the University of Salamanca, in Spain, a colleague of mine gave me a tour of the library. There were thousands of books, far more than Ben-Yehuda's room held, most of them elegantly bound. The collection included incunabula that once belonged to Nebrija, as well as manuals in Latin, dictionaries, and essays and dialogues on all matters connected to language. The sight made me tremble. "This is the cradle of Spanish," I told myself. The way I felt when I saw Ben-Yehuda's library was just the opposite. Is it possible that in this meager library such a far-reaching revolution could have been kindled? Granted, Nebrija was a member of the Iberian aristocracy. He was supported in his linguistic endeavor by the Spanish crown. His *Gramática de la lengua castellana* was dedicated to Isabella, the Catholic queen.

The opposite was true for Ben-Yehuda. Not only did he come from Lithuania, an impoverished corner of the world, but he was a member of a marginalized religious minority with little muscle among the European elite. His journey to Palestine was made precariously, its only incentive the ideological fire that burned in Ben-Yehuda's heart. Even the pursuit of money to subsidize the various volumes of his dictionary had been an ordeal. It took Eliezer and Hemda Ben-Yehuda years to scrape together enough money for the first few. In the end, his edition of the dictionary was left unfinished not only for lack of time but also because the seed money he needed was so hard to secure.

The other important site in Ben-Yehuda's biography that I was able to find was his house in Jerusalem. My wife, Alison, had lived in various places the Middle East in the summer of 1981. Her apartment in Jerusalem had not been far from Me'ah Shearim, the Orthodox neighborhood in what was once called "the New City." It looked onto an Ethiopian church. This was the same street where Ben-Yehuda and his family had lived around 1917. In those days it was called Abyssinian Street. According to St. John, the house was close to the British and Danish consulates, the Hebrew Orphanage, and the American archaeology school. Alison had told me exactly where to look. She remembered a plaque marking the spot.

There's an affecting scene in *Tongue of the Prophets* by Robert St. John that takes place in 1910. The Ben-Yehuda family had just moved in. The children liked the house because it had windows with colored glass. Everyone assembled at the dinner table:

Ben-Yehuda sat flanked by his two sons. At the other end of the long table sat "the Greeks," as Hemda and her daughters were called because they had taken to wearing sandals and long flowing robes of white, yellow, or blue, cut along classical lines.

One day [his son] Ehud said:

"What's the matter, Mother Worry!?"

Hemda smiled. She had grown accustomed to the nickname her own children had given her. Each time they called her by that name she would unconsciously put a hand to her forehead and try to smooth out the wrinkles.

I've quoted this episode in English, but, of course, it took place in Hebrew. It was in this house that Ben-Yehuda consolidated his domestic domain: Mother Worry was teased by her children and made a melodramatic statement, all in a language that had lain dormant only a couple of decades before.

The house on Abyssinian Street was also where, when a number of German-Jewish entrepreneurs financed a technical school in Haifa that would have German as its official language of instruction, Ben-Yehuda and the leading Zionist educator David Yellin orchestrated a campaign to oppose the project. Classes for Jewish children in Palestine needed to be taught in Hebrew, they believed; German, French, and Russian were foreign tongues.

And this was the house Ben-Yehuda lived in when the Balfour Declaration was issued, encouraging a Jewish State in the Holy Land. Then the San Remo Conference took place, giving Britain a mandate over the Holy Land. Afterward, the high commissioner, Sir Herbert Samuel, declared that henceforth there would be three official languages in Palestine: English, Arabic, and Hebrew.

Finally, this was the house where, while World War I was unfolding in Europe, Ben-Yehuda worked on volumes 4 and 5 of his dictionary (the first three had already been released), not only shaping the pool of words on each page but seeking support from publishing houses and financiers.

These events transformed Ben-Yehuda's life, making his objective more tangible. But this home also saw a difficult period. In 1917, Ben-Yehuda and Hemda traveled to the United States. Finances were precarious. When they returned, their house was occupied by strangers. According to St. John, Ben-Yehuda's library was intact because the door to his study had been double-locked. But much of the rest of their possessions were gone, including furniture and kitchen utensils. Moshe Nissim, Ben-Yehuda's secretary, said that he had been forced to sell the items to pay for food. For years to come, members of the family as well as acquaintances would remember it as having been one of the most comfortable places they had ever stayed.

Map in hand, Nowodworski and I took a taxi to Ben-Yehuda's street. Once we were dropped off, the two of us walked up and down several times but were unable to locate the site. No sign of the house was to be found. The plaque that Alison remembered was gone. Nothing remained to mark Ben-Yehuda's presence roughly a century ago. It's as if history had erased him and his family altogether.

Most of the passersby were religious Jews. Every time I

asked if they knew where the reviver of Hebrew had lived, they looked at me as if I were speaking Mandarin.

I was about to give up the search when Nowodworski asked a tourist guide who had just brought his group to the Ethiopian church. It was he who showed us the place—and the site where the plaque Alison remembered had once stood. The guide said the plaque was destroyed by Orthodox Jews still angry with Ben-Yehuda for having taken Hebrew from the Bible into the streets. "He made it mundane," the guide said to his group of Asian tourists. "According to the rabbis, Hebrew was created even before the world. God used it as His blueprint in creating everything. You can imagine why the religious Jews are unhappy. They are proud of their divine language, *lashon ha-kodesh*."

I looked at the silhouette the plaque had left on the wall and felt a pang of sadness. Wasn't Hebrew in Israel everyone's tongue, Orthodox and otherwise? Hadn't the State initiated a new period in Jewish history that was about unity?

A Japanese tourist was standing in front of the wall where the plaque had been. A relative was taking a picture of the sightseer. Nowodworski whispered in my ear, "Israel as a tourist heaven. A dream come true?"

ט

The incident with the plaque on Abyssinian Street—now called Ethiopian Street—prompted me to find out more about language policy in Israel. I had been told that the most

experienced person on the topic was Professor Bernard Spolsky, who for years taught at Bar-Ilan University, where he
was also an administrator. He was the coauthor of an important book titled *The Languages of Israel: Policy, Ideology, and
Practice* (1999) that addresses the issue. He was also the editor of the academic journal *Language Policy*, dedicated to
exploring the ways languages are established and the connection they have with power. Originally from New Zealand,
Spolsky has been an adviser to the Israeli government about
the nation's language policy. I decided to pay him a visit.
The echoes of my encounter with him would reverberate
throughout my pursuit of Ben-Yehuda.

Professor Spolsky lives in Jerusalem, in a spacious apartment in the Jewish Quarter. To get there one needs to traverse the crowded *shuk*, as the Arab market is known,
resisting the constant solicitations of vendors offering all
kinds of merchandise: exotic spices, incense, fresh-squeezed
orange juice, kaffiyehs, soccer balls and jerseys, kitschy
drawings of Bedouins with camels, and all sorts of religious
souvenirs (crucifixes, Stars of David, and replicas of the
Dome of the Rock, the Western Wall, and the Church of the
Nativity). The place feels like a labyrinth in a James Bond
movie. In 1967, after the Six-Day War, Jerusalem was reuni-
fied by Israel. The Jewish Quarter quickly acquired an altogether different aesthetic, Orthodox mothers now pushing
strollers while half a dozen kids rotate around them. Even
so, it doesn't feel as packed as it did before the Six-Day War.
Substantial amounts of money have gone into updating the
architecture. From the outside, the stone walls look clean.
There are staircases going up and down, which yeshiva boys,

wearing fedoras, white shirts, and black pants, and carrying volumes of the Talmud under their arms, traverse at full speed.

The Jewish Quarter is dramatically different from what Ben-Yehuda saw upon his arrival to Israel. He belonged to the do-it-yourself generation. There was no wood, no bricks, no cement-and-machinery construction at the turn of the twentieth century, at least not among Jews. "No one who has only been to Jerusalem in recent years can imagine the desolate appearance of that square in front of the Jaffa Gate at the time of my arrival," Ben-Yehuda wrote. "All those splendid buildings that meet your eyes now on either side of the square and above, up to the 'Moskovia' [the Russian Compound], had not yet been built." In other words, what he saw was a place in desperate need of redemption. And the Zionists were there to implement it.

However, the city appeared to be taken over not by Jews from Eastern Europe or the Levant but by gentiles. In *A Dream Come True*, Ben-Yehuda first described Jerusalem as "destroyed and utterly humiliated," left to the apathy of its inhabitants. But as he approached a series of shops, he was baffled by the construction going on before him. "I asked my escorts to whom these shops belonged and who was doing the renovations, and they told me that the whole site, and the contiguous building, belonged to the Armenian patriarchate, and it was they who had started of late to build houses in something of the European style. I was not happy the gentiles were building Jerusalem, and I said so to my wife with a tone of regret." Obviously, Ben-Yehuda admired the wealth and power of the Armenians. He also felt envious. He adds that the emissaries tried to console him by saying, " 'It doesn't matter. They are building for us. When the Redeemer comes—may it be speedily, in our days—all these buildings will be ours.' " With the war of independence in 1948, the Jerusalem Ben-Yehuda wrote about in his memoir would be resurrected as the Jewish capital.

I was grateful to Professor Spolsky for receiving me. I had imagined him to be a devout scholar with a rabbi's beard and *peyes*. I had thought that his place would be stuffed with religious paraphernalia, that it would be filled with an entourage of pupils and family members. The fact that he had asked me to come to his home and not meet him at his university office suggested that he wanted to talk to me about Jewish tongues on his own turf. But as soon as Professor Spolsky opened the door, I understood how mistaken I had been. It looked like an Upper East Side apartment with an enviable vista of the Holy City: comfortable sofas, Indian-looking tapestries as decoration, a high-definition TV, a shelf filled with CDs along with books on linguistics and demographics.

In his mid-seventies, Professor Spolsky looks like the neurologist Oliver Sacks. His English still retains the melodies of his native New Zealand. After introducing myself as "an Eliezer Ben-Yehuda fan" and explaining that I was eager to understand the way Hebrew in Israel has altered its horizons in the last couple of decades, I asked Professor Spolsky to explain to me the difference between the language as a religious implement, which is what it had been for centuries in the Diaspora, and the language as a secular medium, which is what it has become in modern Israel. I recalled for him the moment that Saul Bellow chronicled in the introduction to his anthology *Great Jewish Short Stories*, published in 1963, thirteen years before he received the Nobel Prize for Literature. Bellow said that in Jerusalem a while back he had had an amusing and enlightening conversation with the dean of Hebrew writers, Shmuel Yosef Agnon.

> This spare old man, whose face has a remarkable youthful color, received me in his house, not far from the barbed wire entanglements that divide the city, and while we were drinking tea, he asked me if any of my books had been translated into Hebrew. If they hadn't been, I had better see to it immediately, because, he said, they would survive only in the Holy Tongue. His advice I assume was only half serious. This was his witty way of calling my attention to a curious situation. I cited Heinrich Heine as an example of a poet who had done rather well in German. "Ah," said Mr. Agnon, "we have him beautifully translated into Hebrew. He is safe."

Bellow's concluding comment, I told Professor Spolsky, was revealing. He wrote that "Mr. Agnon feels secure in his ancient tradition. But Jews have been writing in languages other than Hebrew for more than two thousand years. The New Testament scholar Hugh J. Schonfield asserts that parts of the Gospels were composed in a sort of Yiddish Greek, 'as colorful in imagery and metaphor as it is often careless in grammatical construction.' "

Professor Spolsky said that Agnon's comment was a mystical one held by only a fraction of the Jewish population in Israel.

"Surely not the religious community," I said.

"No, in general the Orthodox are allergic to contemporary Hebrew. In their eyes, it's a debasement, a kind of prostitution of the divine tongue."

"What kind of Hebrew do they speak with one another?" I asked.

"It depends on the persuasion of the particular group one is talking about and the extent to which that group engages Zionist principles. A sect affiliated with a brand of Hasidism from Bratzlav, for instance, employs a speech unlike their counterparts rotating around a rabbi from Nemirov. Overall, they engage in code mixing: Yiddish and Hebrew and English are all juxtaposed. In Me'ah She'arim, one might hear Yiddish intertwined with Hungarian. But nowadays the parlance of the young in that community registers more Anglicisms than anything else."

I asked if there's a difference between the Hebrew spoken by religious Jews and secular Jews.

Professor Spolsky said that there was, but, because of the self-imposed segregation in which the religious community lives in Israel, not enough is known about its verbal idiosyncrasies. "There's deep skepticism toward scientists," he said. "It isn't easy to make a linguistic survey."

On a nearby terrace, a few Orthodox children were playing. The sun was setting in Jerusalem and, as is always the case, it dressed up the stone structures in a cinematic orange tone. At that time of day, I always feel as if I'm in a postcard.

I asked Professor Spolsky to describe the linguistic landscape of Israel for me. He gave a copy of an article he published in the handbook *Sociolinguistics* and an offprint of a piece he cowrote in the book *Corpus Linguistics and Modern Hebrew* about spoken Israeli Hebrew, where he states that Israeli society is made up of a variety of groups that differ from one another by factors such as origin, ideology, language, and religion. The majority of the trustworthy data available on the topic was from the nineties, he said, when there were approximately 4.5 million Hebrew speakers. For about half a million of them it was a second language. The second most frequently used language in Israel at the time was Palestinian Arabic, with 910,000 speakers. (Some 1.6 million speakers of Palestinian Arabic lived in Gaza and the West Bank.) In descending scale, the other languages in use were Russian (800,000 speakers), Judeo-Arabic (485,000 speakers, which included those using Moroccan Judeo-Arabic, Iraqi Judeo-Arabic, Yemeni Judeo-Arabic, Tunisian Judeo-Arabic, and Tripolitanian Judeo-Arabic), Romanian (250,000 speakers), Yiddish (215,000), and onward with French (200,000), English among first-language users (100,000), followed by Ladino, Polish, German, Judeo-Persona (Dzidi), Hungarian, Amharic, Bukaric, Judeo-Georgian, Judeo-Tat (Juhuri), Judeo-Neo-Aramaic, Bulgarian, Turkish, Indian languages, Tigriña, Italian, Israeli Sign Language, Portuguese, Circassian (Adyghe), Armenian, Dutch, Greek, Serbian, Czech, Judeo-Berber, Aramaic, and Judeo-Greek (Yevanic).

"The Tower of Babel all over again," I said.

He smiled. "But the Tower of Babel is a cautionary tale. Monolingualism has never been a feature in Jewish life. Having multiple languages has been an asset in the Diaspora. But it has made it difficult to bring the Jewish people together."

I told Professor Spolsky that in East Los Angeles I had come across a bumper sticker that read MONOLINGUALISM IS CURABLE.

"With the Jews it has never been an ailment—America being an exception, of course," he replied. He added that while Hebrew might be the hegemonic language in Israel, English and Arabic also have an official status.

Moreover, English is becoming a threat to Hebrew. As evidence, Spolsky noted that some years ago the Israeli Supreme Court had legislated that street signs must be displayed legibly in three languages: Hebrew, Arabic, and English.

I asked if the dwellers of the Davidic kingdom had been monolingual. He excused himself for not being a historian but said he doubted it. Canaanite, Chaldean, Moabian, Aramaic, and an array of other tongues were spoken in the desert.

Professor Spolsky told me that Arabic speakers in Israel use different dialects to maintain their identity and build a sense of community. While a single standard variety was employed for literary and formal use, several vernaculars were accepted as spoken languages. He told me about how Arabic speakers in the country don't use the same syntax that their counterparts in Syria, Lebanon, Egypt, Iran, and Iraq use, which often results in their being ridiculed as primitive. He emphasized that in Israel today Hebrew speakers show little interest in learning Arabic.

He argued that Arabs in Israel recognize the need to learn Hebrew in order to advance their status, at least at the economic level, but they lack the opportunity to learn it properly and resist using it. This contrasts sharply with the state's policy of asking new Jewish immigrants to learn Hebrew quickly and give up their mother tongue. In a paper he coauthored in 2003, Spolsky wrote that "the integration of a non-Jewish minority raises serious issues concerning the character of the Jewish State." He stressed that there is a conflict between a willingness to tolerate Arab language maintenance and an effort to discourage Jewish immigrants from loyalty to their home languages. Professor Spolsky concluded that although "most Jews from Middle Eastern countries spoke various dialects of Arabic as their first language, they were discouraged from maintaining that language. Furthermore, second- and certainly third-generation Israelis do not have any proficiency in their original languages." It didn't seem as if he were saying that Israeli Arabs should be forced to learn Hebrew and abandon Arabic, but at times the tone of his comments left me with that impression.

"Arabic has a questionable status in Israel," he commented. "Ever since the arrival of the First Aliyah, Arabic has been seen as a nonpractical tongue. But Hebrew wasn't yet an option, either. It is estimated that in 1881–82 and 1903, between twenty-five and thirty-five thousand Jews made their way to Palestine, mostly from Yemen and Eastern Europe. Hebrew was only spoken by a small bastion of idealists led by Eliezer Ben-Yehuda. The language didn't take hold immediately. He benefited from grants from the Zionist Organization of America, Baron Edmond de Rothschild, and other sources. And he got help from the teachers employed by the Hilfsverein der Deutschen Juden, a German-Jewish support organization with global connections. German was a dominant language of instruction at the time. And the Alliance Israélite Universelle, too, was involved in the effort. It wasn't until the Second Aliyah, which took place between 1904 and 1914, that Hebrew took hold. This wave brought approximately forty thousand Jews, mostly Russian. By 1916, a census indicated that forty percent of the population in the *yishuv*, not including the Orthodox, spoke Hebrew.

"In retrospect," said Spolsky, "it strikes me that that aliyah must have been admirably disciplined. To have embraced a strange, incomplete tongue, one signaling their biblical heritage but still in the process of formation as a vehicle of modern communication, when the hardship of daily life (building nascent communes, working an arid soil, battling an unwelcoming environment) begged for relaxation, seems like a season in Dante's Purgatory.

" 'A purgatory of their own making,' it should be said."

The point was well taken. I had read in historical sources that in 1914 the Hilfsverein was in charge of some fifty schools in the *yishuv*. This translated into seven thousand students. I commented on how tough it must have been for Ben-Yehuda, given the linguistic tension that existed between German Jews (who perceived themselves as the enlightened upper class) and the Yiddish speakers in the Pale of Settlement (seen as uneducated and more pedestrian), to make partnerships with the Hilfsverein and the Alliance. This Kulturkampf, this cultural fragmentation, troubled him deeply. In the eyes of the teachers, Ben-Yehuda represented the very stereotype he was hoping to debunk.

Professor Spolsky made a point of stressing the relevance of Russian in Israel today, especially since glasnost. Although the Soviet Union had a stringent policy of forbidding Jews to leave, every so often there would be a crisis and a small number would arrive, amid much controversy, in the Jewish State. After the fall of the Soviet Union, Jews continued to arrive. Eventually, more than a million Russians made their way to Israel. Their impact on Israeli society was tremendous. One could feel it in every aspect of Israeli life. There were Russian scientists, doctors, academicians, and politicians exerting influence, among them Natan Sharansky. Spolsky said that during elections, signs and advertisements regularly appeared in Russian.

I told Professor Spolsky that not long ago I had gone to see a play in Tel Aviv performed bilingually—some nights the show was in Hebrew, some nights it was in Russian—but the cast did not change. The actors were equally comfortable in both tongues. The troupe could attract an audience in both. Professor Spolsky responded that unlike previous waves of newcomers, Russians seemed to be keeping their mother tongue. "There are approximately a million of them. Israelis are nurturing resentment toward them. It's a response to their condescending attitude toward Israel. The Russians tend to look at the nation's culture as inferior to their own, more superficial."

I mentioned to Professor Spolsky that in Mexico I had been in contact with speakers of Ladino, the language of Sephardic Jews from Beirut and Damascus. They had arrived in the forties. Their connection with Ashkenazic Jews at the time was minimal. I told him that I had gone to the Yidishe Shule. All this exposure to a variety of Jewish ways of communication, I said, had made me curious about—to paraphrase William James—"the varieties of the linguistic experience" in Jewish history.

Teasing me, he asked if I could list for him the number of Jewish languages I was familiar with.

"What do you mean?" I asked.

"The ones invented by Jews," he replied.

Before I had a chance to respond, he himself was making the list. I was flabbergasted by the range of possibilities. The list can be found in his article in *Sociolinguistics*. He starts with Bukharic (aka Judeo-Tadjik) and Dzudezhmo (Ladino, Judeo-Spanish), then moves to Haketiya (Judeo-Spanish), Judeo-Arabic (Yahudic), and Judeo-Aragonese. Then come Judeo-Aramaic (Kurdit, Hulaulá, Targum, Kurdishic), Judeo-Berber, Judeo-Corfiote (from Corfu), Judeo-Georgian (Gurjuc, Gruzinic), Judeo-Greek (Yevanic), Judeo-Italian, Judeo-Moroccan, Judeo-Persian (Dzidi, Jidi, Parsic), Judeo-Yemenite (Temanic), Judeo-Iranian (Juhuri, Judeo-Tat, Tatic), Judeo-Czech (Knaanic), Neo-Aramaic (Lishanit Targum), Judeo-Provençal (Shuadit), and, of course, Yiddish.

Upon reading the list, I was speechless.

He added: "And did I mention Hebrew?"

I laughed.

"That's Jewish polyglotism for you!" Professor Spolsky affirmed. "Of course, most Jews only know one or two Jewish languages. Most of the time they communicate in non-Jewish tongues. They might be fluent in half a dozen of these."

I described my own grandparents, who among them spoke Hungarian, Polish, Latvian, Russian, Czech, German, and Yiddish. "Maybe that's why a conversation between two Jews can be so enticing," I said. "It's not only that there's much to say. There's an abundance of ways of saying it."

Professor Spolsky said that on a regular day in Jerusalem, he could hear more than three dozen different languages. "Tourists up the count," he joked.

Were some of the Jewish tongues he had listed imaginary?

"Not at all." He said that sociolinguists, while seeing some of them as full-fledged tongues and others as dialects and jargons, emphasized the need "to recognize them as languages in their own right." Professor Spolsky described them as the intracommunity languages.

"For religious reasons," he continued, "the most prestigious Jewish tongues in history are Hebrew and Aramaic. They had been standardized as languages of prayer and study in general since the Talmudic period."

The accumulation of examples Professor Spolsky had offered piqued my imagination. Imagine if I could learn all of these Jewish languages, I mused. I would be the perfect Diaspora Jew.

"Perfection is impossible," he said. "Most of these tongues were oral vernaculars, without a written component. And many of them have been devoured by the passing of time."

I mentioned that a few days back, while walking the streets of Tel Aviv, my friend Eliezer Nowodworski had said insightfully that not since Babylon had all Jews spoken the same tongue.

"I doubt that they did even then. Maybe the same tongue, but with infinite possibilities—what linguists refer to as heteroglossia, the coexistence of distinct varieties within a single linguistic code."

Toward the end of our conversation, Professor Spolsky talked about language policy in Israel.

"The Israeli Ministry of Education supervises twenty-five hundred schools," he asserted. "Two thousand have Hebrew as their language of instruction and five hundred have Arabic. Based on a consolidated document released in the mid-nineties, the policy of the ministry is known as 'three-plus.' Each group is required to learn three languages (Jews: Hebrew, Arabic, and English; Arabs: Arabic, Hebrew, and English). The 'plus' refers to the encouragement by the ministry to learn another home, community, or international language. It's a multilingual policy based on the principle that Israel is made up of various ethnolinguistic groups, that immigrant languages are assets and not liabilities, that languages should be addictive rather than subtractive, that plurilingualism is part of multiculturalism, and that different languages are needed for different purposes."

"Won't that multiplicity end up Balkanizing Israel?" I asked.

"On the contrary," he replied. "It will make it stronger.

Since the Tower of Babel, Jews have benefited from their linguistic genius. Why shouldn't Israel, too?"

Before I left the apartment, Professor Spolsky said something that stayed in my mind: "The linguistic repertoire of a people is a reflection of its inner life." As I said good-bye and reentered the maze of the Jewish Quarter, I wondered to myself: Can the repertoire Professor Spolsky was describing in turn be manipulated to change one's inner life?

ב

Professor Spolsky's comment about the Tower of Babel was on my mind as I went to visit Hillel Halkin. I took a train from Tel Aviv to Zikhron Ya'akov, a former farmers' town that still retains the spirit of the Romanian idealists who founded it in 1882 but that in recent times has become a commuters' town. Set on the hills of the Carmel mountains, it has beautiful landscaped gardens and old-fashioned streets. It still has wooden windows and stone posts. A walk through its cemetery offers a tour of its history from Turkish rule through the War of Independence and the successive years of growth. Haifa isn't too far away.

I stayed for a while in Halkin's house. During a car ride to Gamla in the Golan Heights and to Tel Katzir, the kibbutz I had lived on when I first stayed in Israel, I told Halkin about the dream I had had in which an attractive woman—who at the end became naked—described to me, in a Hebrew I was increasingly unable to understand, a mythical bird called the

Liwerant. He asked me if I knew who the woman was. I told him she reminded me of someone I had fallen in love with more than two decades ago when I lived in Kibbutz Tel Katzir, but I wasn't sure. Our conversation moved into the realm of fabulous creatures in the Bible. There is, for instance, the *reêm*, a word that in the King James Version becomes *unicorn*. It appears in the Pentateuch, in the book of Psalms, and in the book of Job. The Septuagint translates it as *monoceros*, or "one-horned creature."

I mentioned the "cockatrice," a serpent that in Hebrew is called *tsephah* or *tstphôni*. It becomes *adder* in the English version. In Proverbs 23:32, it says that wine "biteth like a serpent, and stingeth like an adder."

Halkin added to the list two other biblical creatures: *Behemoth*, from the book of Job 40:15–24, a word that in Hebrew is the plural for *beast*; and *Leviathan*, a sea monster mentioned in Psalms 74:13–14 and Isaiah 27:1, among other places.

I told him that after my dream I had read widely about imaginary creatures in Jewish literature. The Bible was my main source. But I was also attracted to other invented animals, such as Kafka's *Odradek:*

At first glance it looks like a flat star-shaped spool for thread, and indeed it does seem to have thread wound upon it; to be sure, they are only old, broken-off bits of thread, knotted and tangled together, of the most varied sorts and colors. But it is not only a spool, for a small wooden crossbar sticks out of the middle of the star, and another small rod is joined to that at a right angle. By means of this latter rod on one side and one of the points of the star on the other, the whole thing can stand upright as if on two legs.

Halkin's passion has less to do with fanciful monsters than with human chimeras. He told me about a series of trips he had made, starting with one in 1998 in which he accompanied a Jerusalem rabbi and lost-tribes hunter to China, Thailand, and northeast India. Halkin was returning to the Indian states of Mizoram and Manipur to find out if a Tibeto-Burmese ethnic group living in the area was historically connected to the biblical tribe of Manasseh, as it believed itself to be. (Several hundred members of this group, calling themselves the B'nei Menashe, had converted to Judaism and were living in Israel.)

I could see myself as the member of a lost tribe making my own small return. I felt anxious coming back to Tel Katzir after so many years. It felt like toying with H. G. Wells's time machine. The place had changed dramatically. For one thing, it was no longer a kibbutz. Like others of its kind, Tel Katzir had fallen prey to the swift economic changes implemented by Israeli politicians from the eighties onward, changes that had steered the nation, after a period of financial insolvency, toward an open-market phase. The Socialist experiment of the Israeli labor commune, a source of inspiration for millions around the world, could not survive in a competitive environment. A few kibbutzim had endured. Several days before, along with some friends, I had gone to the premises of Ahava, the apothecary company at the kibbutz Ein Gedi, located on the banks of the Dead Sea. With skin-care products on sale everywhere in the Western world, it was an example of capitalist survival. But the majority of kibbutzim weren't as lucky.

At Tel Katzir the grass was overgrown. Some of the rooms where I had once stayed were now rented to commuters working in nearby towns. As I wandered around, I came across Filipinos, Romanians, and Thais. Some spoke Hebrew with heavy accents that made it difficult for me to understand them. I thought: "Ah, multiculturalism has reached these shores as well."

On the way back to Tel Aviv, Halkin and I talked about the biblical episode of the Tower of Babel in Genesis 11:1–9. I told him that, as I read it, the passage is about arrogance: "Don't be presumptuous or else God will punish you."

Given its impact, the actual story is rather short. In the King James Version it says, "And the whole earth was of one language, and of one speech." Then comes temptation: "And [the children of men] said one to another, Go to, let us make brick, and burn them thoroughly. And they had brick for stone, and slime had they for mortar." The passage continues:

And they said, Go to, let us build us a city, and a tower, whose top may reach unto heaven; and let us make us a name, lest we be scattered abroad upon the face of the whole earth. And the Lord came down to see the city and the tower, which the children of men builded. And the Lord said, Behold, the people is one, and they have all one language; and this they begin to do; and now nothing will be restrained from them, which they have imagined to do. Go to, let us go down, and there confound their language, that they may not understand one another's speech. So the Lord scattered them abroad from thence upon the face of all the earth: and they left off to build the city. Therefore is the name of it called Babel; because the Lord did there confound the language of all the earth: and from thence did the Lord scatter them abroad upon the face of all the earth.

I mentioned to Halkin that not long ago I had come across a midrash in the Talmud (*Sanhedrin* 109a) arguing that the generation involved in building the Tower of Babel lost its chance for a place in the World to Come, becoming monkeys, spirits, and demons. I found the reference remarkable. Such had been the arrogance of that generation that God foreclosed its redemption. But was that generation already Jewish? As a religion, Judaism didn't start until Abraham was called by God to leave his place of origin for the land He had assigned for him. Are those who came before Abraham (Adam, Eve, Cain, Abel, Noah) to be considered pagans? If so, they wouldn't have a place in the World to Come anyhow. But didn't the rabbis decide that the righteous of the earth have a place in the World to Come?

Halkin replied: "I've never read the Tower of Babel story as being one of punishment. God makes men speak different languages not to punish them, but simply to prevent them from ganging up on Him; it's a divide-and-conquer maneuver."

The passage right after the one on the Tower of Babel, in Genesis 11:10–26 and 27–32, offers a catalog of descendants from Shem to Terah, Abraham's father, who, along with Abraham, his wife Sarah, and his nephew Lot (from Abraham's brother), leave the Chaldean city of Ur, where Abraham was born, and settle in Haran. I said to Halkin: "And the passage immediately after, Genesis 12:1–2, contains the mandate to Abraham: 'Now the Lord had said unto Abram, Get thee out of thy country, and from thy kindred, and from thy father's house, unto a land that I will show thee. And I will make of thee a great nation, and I will bless thee, and make thy name great; and thou shalt be a blessing.' Isn't it symptomatic that immediately after human society loses its wholeness, the concept of nation takes hold? Two unassuming Hebrew words in this episode, *lech lecha*, announce the covenant between God and the future Israelites, one forever defining their relationship. Hence, no matter how one looks at it, the episode of the Tower of Babel is a turning point."

I wondered if maybe Israel as a nation ought to be seen as a response to chaos. It agglutinates people around a series of motifs, granting them security. I said, "Only as a nation were the Jews able to survive in the Diaspora."

"Not everyone would agree with you, Ilan," Halkin said. "Throughout their history, the Jews have perceived themselves as both a religion and a people."

"That's because in the Bible, nation and God are intertwined," I replied.

I had heard that archaeologists had found an edifice in ruins, large in dimensions, in a town in the land of Shinar,

Babylonia. It is known as the ziggurat of Marduk. Might it be the Tower of Babel? The term *Babel* might point to Babylon, since etymologically it is linked with the Hebrew word *bilbul*, "confusion," and *le-balbel*, "to confuse." In itself the etymology of the term suggests verbal chaos.

"Is polyglotism not a blessing?" I asked.

"Of course it is," Halkin replied, "not only for the Jews, but for the entire human race. For anyone who loves languages, the more of them that are spoken and written in on the face of the earth the better, and one can only grieve over the rapid extinction in our times of so many languages, each one of which is a precious world in itself. Moreover, the argument that if all men spoke one language, they would understand each other better and get along better, has never made much sense to me. Speakers of the same language frequently don't get along either, and some of the cruelest wars in history, as we know, have been fought between them."

I wasn't so sure. I mentioned to Halkin that the Talmud reckons with the reprimand, as do an endless number of rabbinical sources.

Should multilingualism be castigated? The text itself is perplexing. I pointed out that in *Derashot Ha-Ran*, Rabbi Nissim Ben Reuven Gerondi (aka Ran), a fourteenth-century Spanish scholar, stated: "This has been [the Jewish] experience in our present exile. For when religious persecution began in the territory of Ishmael [i.e., the Muslim nations], its refugees were able to flee to the territory of Edom [i.e., Christian Europe] and from Edom to the territory of Ishmael. And this reinforces us a little in the time of our affliction and servitude." Hence, exile and polyglotism are synonymous. And in an early midrash known as *Tanhuma Yelemmedenu*, drafted in the Middle Ages but not edited until after World War II in Warsaw (and translated by William G. Braude), it is stated:

"Come, let us go down, and there confound their language" (Genesis 11:7). He confounded their language, so that one did not understand the language of the other. The first language they had been speaking was the sacred tongue, by which the world had been created.

So the Holy One said: In this world, because of the impulse of evil, My creatures have been separated and have become divided into seventy languages. But in the time-to-come, all of them will come as one to call upon My Name and worship Me, as is said, "Then I will make the people pure of speech, so that they will all invoke the Lord by name, and serve Him with one accord" (Zephaniah 3:9).

This got us talking about Hebrew as the first (i.e., original) language. I said that for centuries thinkers such as Saint Jerome, Thomas Aquinas, and Emanuel Swedenborg described it as "the original tongue" used in the Garden of Eden, even though the Bible doesn't explicitly state that Adam and Eve spoke it in Paradise. Similarly, Ben-Yehuda's linguistic urge was to dream a paradise where the original language could be returned to its source, where it could become primal again. The Babylonian Talmud (*Sanhedrin* 38b), however, stressed that Aramaic was the Edenic language.

Halkin said that this is not the standard view of the rabbis of the Talmud, most or all of whom would have voted for Hebrew as Adam and Eve's language, as is stated in other Talmudic and midrashic passages.

"Yet Dante Alighieri argued that Jesus Christ spoke Hebrew, too," I said. "In the mythical Florence of the thirteenth century, he believed that the Jews were 'the sons of Heber,' and so they were 'called Hebrews after him.' This might be a folk etymology, but Dante adds that 'it remained their particular possession after the confusion of the Tower of Babel, so that our Savior, who was their descendant in his humanity, might use a language of grace and not of confusion.' "

In another conversation in which we talked about Mel Gibson's movie *The Passion of the Christ*, Halkin stressed to me that Jesus spoke Aramaic. He added: "The Jews of Palestine underwent a process of partial Hellenization whose origins go back to Alexander the Great's conquest of the eastern Mediterranean in the fourth century B.C.E. Thousands of Greek and Latin words were borrowed by the Palestinian Hebrew of the period."

Halkin was right. Later, I read Ralph Marcus's insightful discussion on the topic, where he states, for instance, that when the rabbis ordered, after the war of Quietus in 117 C.E., that no father should teach his own children Greek, the word they used to make reference to this war wasn't the Hebrew term *milhamah* but the Greek *polemos*. And when a Palestinian rabbi delivered a sermon mentioning "the chair of Moses," which is a fixture in the architecture of a synagogue, to refer to "chair" he used the Greek word *kathedra*.

Halkin didn't want to leave room for confusion. "It isn't impossible that Jesus might have picked up a smattering of Greek," he said, "but it certainly wouldn't have been his first language or the language in which he spoke to his family, friends, and disciples, and it's unlikely that he would have known it well. Yet there's no debate about it. He spoke Aramaic, which, along with Greek, was one of the two languages spoken in Palestine in his age. Among Jews, a good knowledge of Greek was limited to the upper classes, to which Jesus clearly did not belong. A number of words and phrases attributed to him in the New Testament—such as his *Eli, Eli, lama sabachtani* on the cross—are in Aramaic, at times with some Hebrew (which he would have known from his studies) mixed in."

I said, "I'm talking about deliberate misconceptions. Dante didn't have the scientific information available today. His views in the *Divine Comedy* are based on allegory. And his approach to Hebrew is similar. He sees it as the original language, not because it was in historical time but because, for the Florentine, something always has to come first. The realm of legend has colored Hebrew for centuries. Legend has it that when he sailed across the ocean blue, Christopher Columbus—himself a possible descendant of Jews—brought along with him in the *Niña*, the *Pinta*, and the *Santa María* the converso Luis de Torres, known to be fluent in Hebrew. His skills, it is said, were put to use when communicating with the aboriginal population in the New World, believed to be related to the Ten Lost Tribes of Israel. In addition, Hebrew has survived endless vicissitudes. Where today might one find Akkadian, Syriac, Ugaritic, Moabite, Naba-taean, Amorite, Chaldean, and Phoenician? My view is that those languages never had a theopolitical justification, even though every tongue has its own myth of origins."

I recited to Halkin a line of the oft-quoted letter from Voltaire to Catherine the Great: "I am not like a lady at the court of Versailles, who said: 'What a great shame that the bother at the tower of Babel should have got language all mixed up; but for that, everyone would always have spoken French.'"

כ

Halkin and I stopped at a pleasant restaurant on the banks of the Sea of Galilee for a simple meal of fish and fresh salad. While we dined, I asked him if he thought Eliezer Ben-Yehuda would be happy about the way Israelis use Hebrew today.

"I think Ben-Yehuda would have been dismayed by the state of the demotic Hebrew spoken by most Israelis today," said Halkin. "But he would have been thrilled by the success of the Hebrew revival itself, which is the only case in history of a language dying and being brought back to life again. Demotic usage, after all, changes constantly. I don't believe that Ben-Yehuda would have despaired of today's Hebrew, no matter how clumsily it is spoken by the average Israeli."

When I mentioned the absence of Yiddish books in Ben-Yehuda's personal library, Halkin wasn't surprised. "An extreme anti-Yiddishism was widely prevalent in Hebraist and Zionist circles starting with the *Haskalah* in eighteenth-century Europe, and continuing at least up to World War II and the establishment of the State of Israel," he said. "After that, the animus toward Yiddish disappeared because the war was over. Hebrew had won and Yiddish had lost."

I told him about the thought-provoking intellectual tour that Angel Sáenz-Badillos had given me in his Cambridge office. The topic of the ancestry of Hebrew immediately attracted Halkin. "The ancestry is the subject of intense academic debate," he said.

I told Halkin that Sáenz-Badillos had sent me back to a passage in Herodotus's *Histories*. What Herodotus was after was a thorough understanding of the way different cultures work and how they define themselves vis-à-vis their neighbors. The specific passage that had captured my attention dealt with baby babble. It made me think of Ben-Yehuda's status as a retriever of aboriginal things, his attempt to reach back, in metaphorical terms, to the childhood of Israel as a nation:

[The Egyptian king] Psammetichus, finding that mere inquiry failed to reveal which was the original race of mankind, devised an ingenious method of determining the matter. He took at random, from an ordinary family, two newly born infants and gave them to a shepherd to be brought up amongst his flocks, under strict orders that no one should utter a word in their presence. They were to be kept by themselves in a lonely cottage, and the shepherd was to bring in goats from time to time, to see that the babies had enough milk to drink, and to look after them in any other way that was necessary. All these arrangements were made by Psammetichus because he wished to find out what word the children would first utter, once they had grown out of their meaningless baby-talk. The plan succeeded: two years later the shepherd, who during that time had done everything he had been told to, happened one day to open the door of the cottage and go in, when both children, running up to him with hands outstretched, pronounced the word *becos*. The first time the shepherd made no mention of it; but later, when he found that every time he visited the children to attend to their needs the same word was constantly repeated by them, he informed his master. Psammetichus ordered the children to be brought to him, and when he himself heard them say *becos* he determined to find out to what language the word belonged. His inquiries revealed that it was the Phrygian for "bread," and in consideration of this the Egyptians yielded their claims and admitted the superior antiquity of the Phrygians. That this was what really happened I myself learned from the priests of Hephaestus at Memphis, though the Greeks have various improbable versions of the story, such as that Psammetichus had the children brought up by women whose tongues he had cut out. The version of the priests, however, is the one I have given.

Phrygian is an Indo-European language thought to be, while Herodotus was alive, a "barbaric tongue" as "old as the world." Its users are said to have migrated to Asia Minor, in the region of Bulgaria, around 1200 B.C.E.

I told Halkin that since the children hadn't been socialized yet, Herodotus naively assumed their tongue to be ancestral, much older than his own. "But children are unsystematic," I said. "They don't remember prenatal language; they simply imitate the system of sounds adults use. In other words, Herodotus wants us to believe that language is ancestral."

"This view is partly still in vogue," said Halkin, mentioning the theory, associated most prominently with Noam Chomsky, that a linguistic capacity is inherited. "Most linguists today would probably agree with Chomsky that our brains are in some respects hardwired for language, but they're obviously not wired for any specific language, as Herodotus thought. The whole point of Chomskyan linguistics is to determine what universal rules imposed on us by this wiring enable a normal child to acquire any language on earth with total fluency. Many linguists doubt, though, whether Chomsky has described these rules correctly, and his whole project may yet prove to be a colossal failure."

Aside from its archaeological value, the content of the Torah sheds light on the way the people of Israel understood themselves in linguistic terms. The first reference to speech appears in Genesis 1:3, when, at the very beginning of Creation, "God said [*va-yomer Elohim*]: 'Let there be light.' " The sheer enunciation by the Almighty brings light to darkness.

The other significant passage about language in the Torah, albeit a more tangential one, is used to describe how, as Moses comes down from Mount Sinai with the Decalogue, its laws are passed on to Israel. To understand the multiple implications of this moment, we must look at it against the backdrop of the development of writing systems in Canaan, and in the Near East in general, where cuneiform and hiero-glyphics were the norm in societies with polytheistic reli-gions. The consolidation of Israel as a nation, with Hebrew as its tongue, is directly linked to the monotheistic revolution.

Since the commandments are delivered in Hebrew—in the Bible, at least—the tongue becomes the conduit through which the covenant between God and His chosen people is made. In Exodus 20:2, the Almighty asserts in the first commandment: "I *am* the Lord thy God, which have brought thee out of the land of Egypt, out of the house of bondage" (emphasis added). The stress is on a single deity. Then, in Exodus 20:4, the third commandment is enunci-ated: "Thou shalt not make unto thee any graven image, or any likeness of any thing that is in heaven above, or that is in the earth beneath, or that is in the water under the earth." The statement is God's mandate to abandon idolatry. It might also be understood as an invitation to renounce the forms of writing that used icons.

On the way back to Zikhron Ya'akov, we stopped at a small Mediterranean restaurant and sat on a balcony eating hummus with pita, chewing olives, and drinking wine. I mentioned to Halkin that in Genesis 2:19–20, it says: "And out of the ground the Lord God formed every beast of the field, and every fowl of the air; and brought them unto Adam to see what he would call them: and whatsoever Adam called every living creature [*va-yikra ha-adam shemot*] that was the name thereof. And Adam gave names to all cattle, and to the fowl of the air, and to every beast of the field." I added, "It seems to me that the biblical narrative makes it clear that humans are endowed with the capacity to describe the world around them, to distinguish between animals, and, more important, to invent words. The passage suggests randomness in the human choice of words to name things in the world. This means that Adam, of his own accord, establishes the connection between words and their referents."

ל

Words, words, words . . .

My trip to Israel coincided with the national release of *Milon Ariel ha-Makif,* a magisterial dictionary more than a thousand pages long edited by Maya Fruchtman and Daniel Sivan.

The word *milon,* Hebrew for "dictionary," isn't in the Bible. It was one of Ben-Yehuda's inventions and comes from *milah,* meaning "word." The term in use in Palestine at the dawn of the twentieth century was *sefer milim,* "book of words" (from the German, *Wörterbuch*). Hence, even in an indirect way, every lexicon published in Israel today is indebted to Ben-Yehuda.

But is the debt really substantial?

It was a delight to witness the energy with which the release of *Milon Ariel* was greeted. The volume was displayed in literally every bookstore window. Its content was discussed with enthusiasm—and with the occasional reservation—on TV and radio and in the newspapers. Somehow the fact that another dictionary had been produced seemed to offer Israelis a moment to pause and reflect. Was their language healthy? How had it evolved since the creation of the country in 1948?

I mentioned to Nowodworski that the series of reflections I witnessed amounted to a *siyyum*, the ceremony in which a congregation celebrates the arrival of a new Torah scroll, although the word might also refer to the festivities marking the completion of the study of a Talmudic tractate or a section of the Mishnah.

My synagogue, in Northampton, Massachusetts, had recently acquired a new Torah. The fiesta it threw was moving. The congregation had commissioned a *sofer* in Israel to write the new scroll. When it was finally ready, someone flew to Israel and brought it back. It arrived at the synagogue with the last eighteen letters still unwritten. (The total number of letters in the Torah is 304,805.) In the *siyyum* ceremony, every member of the congregation would help write those last letters with eighteen quills. The shofar was blown, prayers were offered, and the letters were inscribed. Everyone shouted, *"Hazak, hazak, v'nithazek,"* "Strong, strong, and be strengthened," a phrase chanted as the public reading of one of the Five Books of Moses is finished.

Then the study of Torah using the new scroll as conduit

started. For several weeks, that was the scroll used during Shabbat services. People came to see it.

"What's the big deal?" someone asked. "It's identical to the other Torahs."

But it wasn't. The new one was . . . well, new. Or better, it was old and new. It allowed—yet again—for a reappraisal of the covenant between God and the people of Israel.

The arrival of *Milon Ariel*, while prompting a similar explosion of joy, served as an indirect answer to the skeptical member of the Northampton community. Unlike the new Torah, the lexicon was different from its predecessors. It contained new words, new definitions, a new editorial apparatus.

It's no surprise, then, that the Israelis greeting its arrival were anxious. How different was this lexicon from the canonical Even-Shoshan dictionary? Had a large number of Anglicisms been included? How about Russian terms? How does the dictionary approach slang? And what does the Academy for the Hebrew Language have to say about it?

One day soon after the release of *Milon Ariel*, while lying on the beach listening to a call-in radio show, I heard a radio commentator ask: "Would Eliezer Ben-Yehuda be proud?"

A woman called in from Beersheba, the desert city in the Negev where Abraham arrived in the second millennium B.C.E., dug wells, fought the local tribes, and settled down, a fact that serves as evidence of the rights of the Jews to the land of Israel. She said the question was misguided. "Who cares about Ben-Yehuda's *Milon*?" She seemed angry. "Everyone knows it's utterly unusable."

Her reproachful comment prompted me to think about the purpose of dictionaries. They are reservoirs of words old and new from which speakers draw in their daily encounters. Dictionaries are memory banks. They allow us to understand how language has changed over time. Words go in and out of fashion, but the dictionary doesn't discard them, at least not all of them. It leaves them as semantic reminders of how a word has metamorphosed in history. Other dictionaries, prescriptive in nature, have a more overt ideological agenda. Their purpose isn't to mirror the transformations of a language but to dictate the patterns that language must follow. They leave out words, thinking that speakers then won't use them.

Almost fifteen years after Ben-Yehuda's death, Yehuda Gur's lexicon appeared under the aegis of Dvir, a publishing house created by Bialik, among other intellectuals. While still archaic in tone, Gur's lexicon was far more useful to Israelis because of its attempt to reflect their living tongue. Then, in 1947, just before the state's independence, Abraham Even-Shoshan published his magnum opus, still the most authoritative and popular of all, astute in its use of diacritics, with appendixes dealing with grammar. It has been updated repeatedly, most recently in 2004.

Then came the lexicon by Reuven Alkalai, which is like a Larousse: sharp but trustworthy. And there are others, such as the *Milon ha-Hoveh*, under the editorship of Shoshana Bahat, of the Academy of the Hebrew Language, and the scholar Mordekhai Mishor. Theirs stresses what's proper and what isn't, organizing content according to etymological stems and not alphabetically. And the *Milon Rav Milim*, edited by a team led by Yaacov Choveka, methodical in its inclusion of neologisms and technological material (with a popular online version), as well as the *Milon Sapir* of Etan Avne'on, also up-to-date in technological material.

The *Milon ha-Lashon ha-Ivrit ha-Yeshanah v'ha-Hadashah*, Ben-Yehuda's multivolume lexicon, is their ancestor. Only five of the projected seventeen volumes materialized in his lifetime. He worked inexhaustibly on them, at times in eighteen-hour marathons. He was disciplined in his commitment. The results were plentiful. He dug out 335 historical examples of different usages of the word *lo*, "no" in Hebrew, and 210 for the use of the word *ken*, "yes."

His work wasn't the only undertaking keeping him busy. He met Herzl. He befriended Jabotinsky, the founder of the Jewish Legion in World War I as well as the leader of the clandestine Jewish militant organization called Irgun. He was a friend of Israel Zangwill, the British-Jewish author of *Children of the Ghetto* and *The King of Schnorrers* and the person responsible for coining the concept of the melting pot to describe an immigrant society in which newcomers sacrifice their ethnic and religious identity to become part of the mainstream. And Ben-Yehuda traveled: he went to London and Moscow, but, most significant (at least to me, since it makes his ordeal a bit more immediate), he went to New York for research. The trip took place during World War I, just as Jamal Pasha, the Turkish commander in Palestine, outlawed Zionism. That infuriated Ben-Yehuda, but he was tired of fighting political battles. His trip to New York was sponsored by a small committee of wealthy American Jews and was orchestrated with the support of U.S. ambassador to the Ottoman Empire Henry Morgenthau.

Professor Richard James Horatio Gottheil, director of the American School of Oriental Research in Jerusalem, which was just across from Ben-Yehuda's house on Abyssinian Street, arranged for a room in the basement of the New York Public Library where Ben-Yehuda could work. The library's Semitic Department also arranged to supply him with all the books he needed. He traveled to Washington, D.C., as well, to consult material at the Library of Congress. Not only was Ben-Yehuda at work on the dictionary, the first volume of which had appeared in 1910. He also wrote a book, *Until When Was Hebrew Spoken?* (in the original: *Ad Eimatai Dibberu Ivrit?*). His social life was intense, too. He was at Carnegie Hall when a celebration presided over by U.S. Supreme Court justice Louis D. Brandeis took place to applaud the naming of a British high commissioner for the British Mandate in Palestine. He went to hear Enrico Caruso at the Metropolitan Opera, and was wined and dined by prominent American Jews. In fact, such was his appeal that just before he returned to Palestine, in February 1919, the Histadrut, an organization for the promotion of Hebrew culture, handed him a check for $10,000, which, according to St. John's biography, was to be "used to build a house in Jerusalem in which he could work peacefully the remaining years of his life."

Before Ben-Yehuda's time, Hebrew lexicons were organized around etymological stems. The approach seemed inefficient to Ben-Yehuda. He wanted to produce a book that organized the words alphabetically, not by stem. But his quest wasn't to describe the Hebrew expressions he found in the Bible. Zionist ideology played a major role. Only the words that he trusted could be used needed to be recorded. His objective was to teach immigrants how to speak . . . and how not to. To achieve it, he needed to offer a catalog useful to his people.

Whenever I think of lexicography, the magisterial work of Samuel Johnson comes to mind. This is rather absurd, given that lexicography has undergone a dizzying transformation in the last 150 years. From an exercise that began in the West with Hesychius of Alexandria's sophisticated lexicon of more than fifty thousand entries, the work of devotees as diverse as Pierre Larousse, María Moliner, Eric Partridge, Noah Webster, Vladimir Dal, and even J. R. R. Tolkien has made the discipline more heterogeneous. Compiling a lexicon is a rigorous task, with specific rules.

Technology has changed the landscape. Today the use of software allows companies such as Larousse and Merriam-Webster to handle large amounts of data with precision. Compared to them, Samuel Johnson was a mere amateur. An eighteenth-century polymath, he was a journalist and newspaper columnist, an editor of Shakespeare's work, a scholar of English literature, and a traveler with an endless curiosity for the history of places and a propensity for big meals. *A Dictionary of the English Language*, his superb lexicon, on which he worked from 1745 to 1755, was the result of a personal interest and, thus, not an academic project in the traditional sense. Literacy in England was on the rise. Likewise, the printing-press industry was expanding. Realizing the scope of these changes, Johnson improvised himself as a lexicographer. He didn't go to either Oxford or Cambridge. Instead, he was a self-taught gentleman whose voracious learning turned him into a walking encyclopedia.

Some of his definitions are deliciously idiosyncratic. *Oats*, he says, is "a grain, which in England is generally given to horses, but which in Scotland feeds the people." An *orgasm* is a "sudden vehemence." *Bible* is "the sacred volume in which are contained the revelations of God." A *bigot* is "a man devoted to a certain party." And, most celebrated perhaps, a *lexicographer*, Johnson states, is "a writer of dictionaries; a harmless drudge, that busies himself in tracing the original, and detailing the signification of words." In contrast, Ben-Yehuda's definitions are dull. There's an absence of spark in them, a lack of creativity. But that isn't the problem. Unlike Johnson's original purpose, which was to establish the parameters of the English language, Ben-Yehuda's interests lay in recovery. His talent wasn't in defining old words but in inventing new ones that were etymologically sound. Which past words could be refurbished in the present?

Ben-Yehuda's audience wasn't his contemporaries. It was the future citizen of the Jewish State, a Hebrew speaker not yet born. Still, in his *Milon* he made questionable decisions. His sources were the Torah, the Talmud, and Rabbinic literature. He focused only on words of Semitic origin, leaving out terms in Aramaic and words of other origins. He didn't seek help from around the Jewish world by notifying people that he was in search of entries, textual references, and bibliographical sources. It's in the area of neologisms that Ben-

Yehuda's work suffers the most. A few show up in Israeli trivia contests today. He coined *saj-rajak* for "telephone," but Israelis simply say *telefon*. Likewise with *makolit* for "gramophone," replaced by *patifon;* and *amunot* for "democracy," replaced by *demokratia*. A famous example is *badura* for "tomato," which Ben-Yehuda took from the Arabic; it was rejected in favor of *agvani'á*, which Naphtali Tur-Sinai had proposed, a word with the stem *ayin, gimel,* and *bet* making reference to carnal love, what the French call *pomme d'amour* and the Italians *pomodoro*.

I asked Hillel Halkin how he views Johnson and Ben-Yehuda. He considers Johnson "a bemused observer of life" and Ben-Yehuda "an engaged actor." It is ideology, he believes, that draws them apart. "Ben-Yehuda was a fighter for a nationalist cause, whereas Johnson, to the best of my knowledge, had no cause at all apart from that of a civilized and gentlemanly cosmopolitanism." But maybe Johnson isn't the right point of comparison. The distance between him and Ben-Yehuda is 150 years. Closer in time (again, in English lexicography, in my eyes the one with the most singular history) are the makers of the *Oxford English Dictionary*. An offshoot of the scientific need to standardize language in the second half of the nineteenth century, Ben-Yehuda's efforts and those of the Oxford dons are more or less concurrent.

The *OED*, a brainchild of London's Philological Society, whose members believed English dictionaries in the mid-nineteenth century were obsolete for an empire undergoing a rapid intellectual expansion, was created by a succession of editors who finally established a connection with Oxford

University, a partnership that gave them economic solvency. The central figure in the shaping of the *OED* was James Murray, a Scottish philologist who was able to orchestrate a worldwide effort involving hundreds of volunteers who collected and sent words and their historical sources on cards to the Scriptorium, as he called his office at Mill Hill School. From beginning to end, Murray's goal was to include *every single word* available in the English language. With the help of his daughters and a cadre of colleagues, he organized the information. The first fascicle was published in 1884. By the time the full edition appeared in 1928, it contained 414,825 words.

The *OED* is a story in universalism. So is Ben-Yehuda's journey. In 1890, he cofounded the Committee for the Hebrew Language, an entity endowed with safeguarding the emergent needs of Hebrew in Palestine at the end of the nineteenth century. Some of his colleagues were David Yellin, A. Y. Brawer, H. A. Zuta, and Joseph Klauser, all pedagogues, philologists, scholars, and journalists concerned with the revival of the sacred tongue. In more than one way, the Committee for the Hebrew Language had the same aspirations as the London Philological Society—but not the resources. Also, the individualism of its members worked against a consensus.

In his autobiography, *A Tale of Love and Darkness*, Amos Oz talks about how his beloved uncle Joseph (Joseph Gedaliah Klausner) coined simple words—"words that seemed to have been known and used forever"—like the ones used in Hebrew nowadays for *pencil, iceberg,* and *shirt.* He was also responsible, according to Oz, for more complex terms, such as those for *monotonous, sensual,* and *rhinoceros.* Clearly, the lexicographic passion was in the air. In his *Milon,* Ben-Yehuda introduced words like *mil'ab* for "sport," from the Arabic stem meaning "to play"; and *offnayim* for "bicycle," from the Hebrew for "wheel" and "two." Wouldn't it have been more advantageous to everyone had the Committee for the Hebrew language agreed to orchestrate a collective effort to make a dictionary, like the *OED,* improved by the sum of individual parts?

Such ideas circulated at the time, but politics made them impossible to realize. Society was fractured into divergent ideologies. A concerted effort might have been possible at a time of peace and with the backing of a wealthy organization. But at the time money was allocated for the relocation of immigrants into the *yishuv* in Palestine and for the defense of the Jewish settlements. What was needed was an army of soldiers, not a battalion of lexicographers. In the end, Ben-Yehuda opted to go his own way, investing his energy in the shaping of his own *Milon.* Robert St. John puts it succinctly in *Tongue of the Prophets:* "better alone than wasted."

But wasted, too, are many of its pages. Sadly, the catalog Ben-Yehuda envisioned was short-lived. Even a superficial look shows the extent to which his choices were misguided: it is stuffed with obsolete words that nobody in Israel has use for today. Indeed, browsing through its pages gives one the feeling of walking through a wax museum filled with figures like Attila the Hun and Cleopatra. They look fake.

מ

To better appreciate the ambivalence Israelis feel toward Ben-Yehuda, I spent some time at Ha-Akademiyah la-Lashon ha-Ivrit, the Academy of the Hebrew Language, on the premises of the Hebrew University, where his desk and other working materials are located. A descendant of Ben-Yehuda's Committee for the Hebrew Language, its mission is to standardize Hebrew. In considering its reach, one might do well to remember a legendary maxim by the Yiddish linguist and founder of the YIVO Institute for Jewish Research Max Weinreich: the difference between a language and a dialect is that a language has an army and a navy behind it. That army and navy is the academy.

Not every modern language has an academy to defend it. The Accademia della Crusca, the Académie Française, and the Real Academia Española, based in Florence, Paris, and Madrid, respectively, have embraced that undertaking. These institutions, some of which date back to the sixteenth century, depend on state money; that is, their budgets come from taxpayers. The Israeli academy, although obviously more recent (it was founded in 1953), functions that way, too.

It would be naive to expect the building housing the Academy to be commanding, for this would serve as indisputable proof that Ben-Yehuda's dream had been turned into reality. Israel is a relatively young nation with limited financial resources. Still, I was surprised to see how small and graceless the structure was in comparison with other federal institutions. Made up of interconnected buildings, its combined size doesn't come even close to that of the cafeteria at the headquarters of Tzahal, Israel's military forces. This impression was confirmed when I heard of the ambitious effort under way in its offices and conference rooms. I had been told that a major historical dictionary was in the making here. But where? Doron Rubinstein, a thirty-three-year-old sabra staff person with an idiosyncratic train of thought, volunteered to be my guide. As I was being taken around, I looked for signs of books, concordances, and computers. I found a few, but for the most part the equipment looked outmoded, or at least unforgivably limited for such an endeavor. Could these facilities house the resources for a lexicon that would address everything about everything that has to do with Hebrew?

What Rubinstein called the Historical Dictionary Project (he used the acronym HDP) stops in 1948, when the State of Israel was created. This means that it doesn't address spoken Hebrew in any fashion, concentrating instead on written texts from the Bible to the Holocaust. I asked him why. "The Academy doesn't need to tackle areas other dictionaries already address," he replied. "Even-Shoshan, for example, is a valuable resource dealing with Israeli Hebrew. There's no need for overlapping."

Rubinstein is a short, bulky man without intellectual pretensions. The day I met him he was wearing a blue T-shirt, casual pants, and sport shoes. He studied Bible and the history of the Hebrew language at Tel Aviv University. Rubinstein explained to me that the Academy has what he calls a scientific secretariat, whose job it is to answer queries from the public on a variety of matters ranging from pronunciation to spelling to suggestions for new words. Several times he emphasized the word *scientific*, as if calling my attention to the Wissenschaft des Judentums, the nineteenth-century movement that sought critical investigation of Jewish literature and culture. The portrait he wanted to draw for me was of a rigorous institution committed to the patient study of every word in Hebrew.

This approach offered a response to the plethora of jokes the Academy generates among Israelis. Nobody takes it seriously. When during a party a few days earlier I had mentioned that I would be visiting it, several people told me it was a dump. "Taxpayers' money could be handled better," a Uruguayan translator said to me. "Does Israel need to have the government protect its language? We can do it on our own. Enough energy is given to protection of other areas. Hebrew isn't being attacked by Islamic fundamentalists, at least not to my knowledge."

I asked Rubinstein if he was aware of the jokes. He grinned. "Who isn't?" He explained it as the refusal of Israelis to be told by anyone how to handle themselves. I wasn't sure if he himself was among the critics. "We like doing things in our own way. Nobody wants to be lectured on what words to use and what words to avoid."

He explained that in response to the rapid changes in technology, the primary business of the Academy is coining new words. He gave several examples of words that the

Academy had proposed and that, after initial trepidation by the public, had been embraced by Hebrew speakers: *caletet*, which the Academy suggested as an alternative to "cassette." And *monit*, a replacement for "taxi," also was endorsed by Israelis.

I knew of numerous other coinages that had been ignored. I mentioned *cornflakes*, which Hebrew speakers use to describe cereal in general, not only the Corn Flakes brand. The Academy had tried to replace it with something more official but had failed. When I asked Rubinstein about such words, he acknowledged their existence but didn't seem ready to discuss their specifics.

My conversation with Rubinstein took place in a crowded office he shared with a colleague. There were piles of photocopies on a large central table, as well as several chairs made unusable by open books, reference works, and other material. On the bookshelf were a handful of lexicons. He sometimes looked at them as if to argue his point, telling me that the Academy was involved in compiling a data bank of Hebrew children's names. "It already has some ten thousand entries," he stated.

He said that the Academy is subdivided into committees handling transliteration, orthography, and grammar. It also publishes glossaries and books connected to its mission. There are glossaries of words in various disciplines—zoology, dentistry, engineering, and artificial intelligence, among others. The best-selling one is on medicine. I was shown the publications dealing with punctuation. One booklet was on unvocalized Hebrew, another covered the Romanization of Hebrew, a third contained transliterations from the Roman alphabet to Hebrew. "The Academy publishes scholarly studies on an array of topics, such as the syntax of Midrashic Hebrew, the Babylonian Masora, the Hebrew components of Yiddish, and the evolution of spoken Hebrew in pre-State Israel," said Rubinstein.

He introduced me to Orly Albeck, a tall woman who worked as one of the Academy's secretaries. She told me that the members in charge of coining terms use their own scholarly knowledge and the database that has been collected for years to find suitable terms that they propose to the general public. "It works as the Sanhedrin did in Roman times," she said, making reference to the assembly of twenty-three Jewish judges of ancient Israel that constituted the Supreme Court and legislative body. "The Academy has twenty-three members. The new members are nominated by the current ones, who vote them in. It's important to have a foot in every walk of life in Israel. Candidates include linguists, intellectuals, writers, and so on. Everyone works on a volunteer basis."

I asked Albeck what the gender ratio was.

"Twenty-one men and two women," she answered.

"Is that the same ratio found among the secretaries and other staff?"

"No, no, no. There are far more women on staff than men." She added: "Just as in top-level strata of the army."

"Are there any Arab members in the Academy?"

"No," said Albeck. "It's a small operation."

Next on my agenda was a meeting with the current editor of the HDP and vice president of the Academy, Abraham

Tal, an emeritus professor in the Department of Hebrew and Semitic Studies at Tel Aviv University. In his mid-seventies, Professor Tal is a small, fragile man with a friendly demeanor. He reminded me of a Yiddish teacher I had at the Yidishe Shule. That day Professor Tal was wearing a jacket and tie, an anomaly in Israeli office fashion, which is generally low-key.

He said that shortly after the founding of the Academy, the president at the time pushed to take up a previous suggestion: creating a lexicon that would go beyond Ben-Yehuda's effort. The initial step was to locate all the Hebrew texts from the postbiblical period on in order to compile detailed catalogs. Computers are used today, but I'm not quite clear as to their level of sophistication.

Professor Tal stressed that the HDP has been in the works for years. There's no end in sight for it. It will be etymological, offering the historical roots of a word. It will start with biblical Hebrew and continue through Rabbinic times, onward to 1948. Identifying the sources was tremendously arduous: every single text in the entire Jewish Diaspora needed to be passed through a sieve. Professor Tal explained to me that the HDP has two lexicographical sections: the Ancient Literature Section and the Modern Literature Section. Doron Rubinstein, he said, was in charge of coordinating the latter. There was also the Computer Section, which is involved in digitizing each section's data and creating a database for each. He referred me to the website of the Academy, where it says that, initially, each literary work is typed (it doesn't say scanned) into the computer. The text is then broken down into words, and a dictionary entry is created for each one. On the basis of the lexical entries, a database is created in concordance form, containing all the literary contexts in which the entry word occurs, in chronological order. The composers of the lexical entries for the dictionary-in-the-making utilize the database in order to choose the most appropriate examples to illustrate each word's meaning.

I asked Professor Tal to give me an example. He again pointed me in the direction of the Academy's website, where the Hebrew stem *ayin*, *reish*, *bet* is offered. It made reference to a sample entry that was seventy-five pages long (without indexes and statistical data).

"A seventy-five-page entry is huge," I said. "What use can it be to the average Hebrew speaker who is just looking for the quick definition of a word?"

He argued that the finished lexicon, whenever it appeared, would be monumental in its dimensions.

"We envision the Academy as a national lexicographical center of Hebrew," he announced. "The HDP needs to be updated regularly."

I asked what has been done so far. Professor Tal responded that currently 540 treatises of varying length had been entered into the computer. These represent the works of 71 authors and comprise some 8,852,000 words. A computerized dictionary of concordances of more than 200 treatises containing some 3,047,000 words had been compiled.

"Should we expect the HDP soon?"

He was silent.

"Will the Messiah be carrying it under his arm?"

"Hopefully it will be here before then."

I wanted Professor Tal to discuss slang, so I made sure that before visiting the Academy offices I had met the Israeli authority on the subject: Reuven (aka Ruvik) Rosental. He's a celebrated journalist, editor, and one of Israel's foremost commentators on language use and abuse. (He writes a weekly column for *Maariv* called, in a loose translation, "The Language Arena.") When he was in his twenties, Rosental lived on Kibbutz Nachshon. He studied linguistics and philosophy at Tel Aviv University, then turned to journalism. He is now in his fifties.

His claim to fame comes from the 2005 publication of a dictionary of Israeli slang. The dictionary has been celebrated by the media, but academics have criticized it for being put together carelessly and containing more than its fair share of typos and errata.

When I told Rosental my reason for visiting Israel, he responded by saying: "But other languages have gone through a revival, among them Catalan, Welsh, and Breton. Why aren't you following their path?" I told him about my dream with the *Liwerant*, about my search for Ben-Yehuda's impact on present-day Israel and on my own intimate connection with the sacred tongue. He explained to me that unquestionably the most important development in Hebrew today was its various vernaculars. Whether one considers the jargon of adolescents, of advertising, of prostitution, of sports, of the military, or any other, each of them manipulates Hebrew according to its needs, making it more resilient but less manageable by academies and other learned institutions hoping to contain it according to their own will. "Hebrew is messy, boisterous, even chaotic," said Rosental.

Rosental is a maverick with little patience for authority. His father died when he was five years old, the same week that his brother Gidon was born. Gidon later died in the Yom Kippur War. He told me that when it comes to language, the function that Tzahal serves in Israel is simultaneously that of a maintainer of standards ("generals are strict in their vocabulary") and a feeder of colloquialisms. He mentioned the term *golani* as an expression referring to the famous Golani Brigade, in which, according to popular belief, soldiers mostly from the Israeli lower class speak a more pedestrian Hebrew. And he reflected on the incommensurable impact of American pop culture on Hebrew, evidenced in the infinite number of Anglicisms. He meditated, too, on the use of acronyms, the equivalent of saying in English ID for identity card, SS for social security number, and ATM for automated teller machine. Rosental said the use of acronyms began as a feature of military parlance and moved to the civilian realm. He gave the example of *zabashkah*, an abbreviated form of *zot hab'aiá shelkhah*, meaning "That's your problem!"

The success of Rosental's slang lexicon took him by surprise. A new edition had already been published and more were being contemplated. "To keep it fresh, I have to be always updating it." It was the same statement Professor Tal later made to me, except that the fascicles of the HDP weren't nearly as popular among Hebrew speakers as Rosental's volume had been.

In fact, Rosental told me that, as a result of his *Maariv* column and the dictionary itself, the Academy of the Hebrew Language had written him letters asking him to ponder a particular definition he had offered. The tone of those letters was archaic. "Nothing fresh in them," said Rosental. "They include lines like 'We have been notified by a third party that recently you've legitimated this or that term.' 'We have been notified'? Don't these old-fashioned erudites read the newspaper? Don't they watch TV? Are they in touch with what's happening with Hebrew at rock concerts, basketball games, in street cafés?"

With Rosental's objections in mind, I asked Professor Tal what role slang played in the HDP.

"The HDP is historical," he replied.

"But there was biblical slang at the time of Ezra. And, as the Dead Sea Scrolls make clear, when Jesus was alive during the Roman control of Palestine, the sect of the Essenes used the vernacular."

"I understand slang to be a spoken language only. If it is recorded in a text, it already has an official imprimatur."

I asked Professor Tal about Rosental, but he didn't want to pursue the topic. I asked him about the fact that, as some linguists suggest, Israelis "slaughter" their language (a recurrent accusation), and that they are lazy and speak not Hebrew proper but something called *Israeli*. For instance, as described by Ghil'ad Zuckermann, a scholar at the University of Queensland, in Australia, for "good-bye" Israelis say *yala bay*, which is an Arabic-English hybrid expression; or they say *eser shekels*, ten shekels, rather than *asarah shkalim*.

Professor Tal smiled when hearing these complaints.

I remembered the famous anecdote told by Zuckermann of the linguist Haim Blanc taking his daughter to see an Israeli production of *My Fair Lady*, based on George Bernard Shaw's play *Pygmalion*. At one point, Professor Henry Higgins, the irascible phonetician, attempts to teach Eliza Doolittle, the flower girl, to properly pronounce the *r* as the alveolar trill used by Sephardic Jews, who are perceived in Israel to be culturally inferior, rather than the Israeli lax uvular approximant that characterizes Ashkenazic Jews. Doolittle says: "The rain in Spain stays mainly in the plain." According to Zuckermann, in Hebrew it came out as *"Barad yarad bidrom sfarad ha-erev,"* that is, "Hail fell in southern Spain this evening." After the show was over, Blanc's daughter asked him why Higgins was trying to teach Doolittle to speak like a cleaning lady.

Professor Tal knew the anecdote. He said he didn't want to sound apologetic. "Israeli Hebrew is a living creature, full of possibilities. It cannot be ruled with an iron sword!" he stated.

I switched gears, asking if Ben-Yehuda might be compared to Dr. Johnson.

His eyes sparkled. "Yes," he replied, "he's a Johnsonian philologist."

His comment pleased me, but it wasn't satisfying. I've always perceived the history of lexicography as driven by mavericks without academic credentials. They are the ones setting the pace. Johnson had been on a crusade against Galicisms, just as Ben-Yehuda wanted to clearly delineate the parameters of the language by eliminating any reference to the non-Semitic past. Still, I understood how treacherous the comparison was. Ben-Yehuda was an ideologist at a time of turmoil. His intellectual efforts had a single purpose: to acknowledge the suitability of a tongue used for Rabbinic debates since the time of the Tannaim, as the compilers of the Mishnah were known. Instead, Dr. Johnson engaged his considerable talents to apprehend the grandiosity of English, which already in Elizabethan times—through commerce, theater, and poetry—had reached unsurpassable heights of sophistication. Yet that language dates back to the Norman invasion in 1066. It's a tongue of kings, soldiers, actors, civil servants, thieves, corsairs, and whores. In Johnson's eyes, philology and morality went hand in hand. In contrast, and as Halkin had said to me, for Ben-Yehuda it was philology and politics.

Toward the end of our dialogue, I told Professor Tal about the ridicule with which Israelis spoke of the Academy and mentioned that I had spoken with Doron Rubinstein about it.

"It's no secret," he responded. He talked about an anti-intellectual trend in Israeli society that led to mistrust of all academic efforts.

I said that in Spain, which I visited frequently, people also kept a distance from the Real Academia Española. They poked fun at it. And yet, deep inside, they appreciated its labors. I asked Professor Tal if the same was true in Israel.

"I don't know," he replied. "Politicians are often proud of

the institution. Whenever Ariel Sharon would sit down to craft a speech for the Knesset, his secretary would call the Academy with grammatical questions. He knew posterity would look not only at what he had said but at how he had said it. Nevertheless, the majority of Israelis are less interested in official approval."

"Is it because language for them isn't legislated from above?" I asked.

"Perhaps."

As a final question, I asked Professor Tal if he believed Israel could do without the Academy.

"Sure. The nation doesn't need it!"

ב

In the evenings, I would return to my hotel, exhilarated yet totally exhausted. My mind would still be spinning as I showered, jotted down notes in my small blue-and-brown notebook, and transcribed some of my conversations. The hotel had a gym and a swimming pool on the top floor. I would swim laps for half an hour, use the sauna, then shower and relax.

I was in the sauna one evening, immersed in my own thoughts, when the door suddenly opened and a naked woman walked in. She was probably in her late twenties. Obviously she hadn't seen me at first; otherwise she wouldn't have sat in one of the corners, between me and the structure holding the hot stones.

Or had she? I was nervous. Should I make a pass? Should I at least alert her to my presence?

Not that I was naked. I was wearing a bathing suit. My towel was hanging outside.

Sweat was running down me. Breathing quietly, I looked at her. Frazzled as I was, sitting in the moist air with a temperature of around one hundred degrees, for a second I thought she looked like the Hebrew-speaking woman in my dream about the *Liwerant*.

When the woman finally noticed me, she was overcome by shame. *"Slikhah,"* she said. *"Slikhah."* And she quickly ran out.

At first I didn't understand what she said. She seemed to have swallowed the last syllable of the word. *Slikhah* in Hebrew means "I'm sorry."

But it sounded to me like *shit*.

ד

I have been a devoted reader of David Grossman ever since I came across his novel *See Under: Love*, a meditation on childhood under the shadow of the Holocaust. The book revolves around the personality of Bruno Schulz, a Polish painter and writer of two slim phantasmagorical books who was shot by a Gestapo officer in his hometown, Drohobycz, in 1942. The fact that Grossman, as an Israeli, tackles Schulz, a quintessential emblem of the Jewish Diaspora, was appealing to me. It showed a kind of debt to Jewishness I found missing in the oeuvre of other contemporary Israeli writers. He and I met for breakfast one morning in the Jerusalem hotel where I was staying.

Grossman talked about Shmuel Yosef Agnon, the figure in the Israeli literary canon who serves as a bridge between the shtetl and the *yishuv*. I said that, having talked to students, teachers, and the average reader, it seemed to me that Agnon no longer had a *living* audience. I stressed the word because I knew that Agnon is the only Israeli writer to have won the Nobel Prize, which he shared with the German poet Nelly Sachs (who was also Jewish) in 1966. And that he was a part of the curriculum in high schools. But, as a young friend put it to me, Agnon was "dry, tedious, an empty classic not in touch with the issues," a chore in course lists. This was bewildering because what makes Agnon interesting to me is the way he beautifully blends Yiddish and Hebrew cultures. His novel *The Bridal Canopy* is an epic about Galician Judaism at the start of the nineteenth century, whereas *Only Yesterday* is set during the period of the Second Aliyah. Agnon's Nobel banquet speech, delivered in Stockholm on December 10, 1966, had been a landmark for the young country. In it he discussed the meaning of prayer, a remarkable thing for a novelist whose country's vernacular had been tempered by secular fire:

> Our sages of blessed memory have said that we must not enjoy any pleasure in this world without reciting a blessing. If we eat any food, or drink any beverage, we must recite a blessing over them before and after. If we breathe the scent of goodly grass, the fragrance of spices, the aroma of good fruits, we pronounce a bless-

ing over the pleasure. The same applies to the pleasures of sight: when we see the sun in the Great Cycle of the Zodiac in the month of Nissan, or the trees first bursting into blossom in the spring, or any fine, sturdy, and beautiful trees, we pronounce a blessing. And the same applies to the pleasures of the ear. Through you, dear sirs, one of the blessings concerned with hearing has come my way.

It happened when the Swedish Chargé d'Affaires came and brought me the news that the Swedish Academy had bestowed the Nobel Prize upon me. Then I recited in full the blessing that is enjoined upon one that hears good tidings for himself or others: "Blessed be He, that is good and doeth good." "Good," in that the good God put it into the hearts of the sages of the illustrious Academy to bestow that great and esteemed Prize upon an author who writes in the sacred tongue; "that doeth good," in that He favoured me by causing them to choose me. And now that I have come so far, I will recite one blessing more, as enjoined upon him who beholds a monarch: "Blessed art Thou, Oh Lord, our God, King of the Universe, Who hast given of Thy glory to a king of flesh and blood." Over you, too, distinguished sages of the Academy, I say the prescribed blessing: "Blessed be He, that has given of His wisdom to flesh and blood."

In Israel the union of cultures, fragile in Ben-Yehuda's era, has fractured still more today. Grossman said that while Orthodox Jews had a growing power in the political spectrum, the nation's literature didn't place them at center stage. The average Israeli writer today is secular. His connection to politics is far more concrete than that of Agnon. This difference is a result of the militarization of the country.

Grossman talked about the role of the Israeli writer in society. He said that, as in South Africa, Eastern Europe, and Latin America, writers are seen less as entertainers than as the nation's conscience. This is quite a task, obviously. It is left to the writer to challenge the assumptions put forth by corrupt politicians, to question the excesses of power, to confront the policies of the State. This needs to be done gracefully.

I told him I had recently read *A Dream Come True*. In it Ben-Yehuda described how, upon arriving in Palestine, he recorded his own choices when it came to religion. He kept a kosher home, attended synagogue, and performed the Jewish rituals. At one point Ben-Yehuda said that he didn't want to be a hypocrite and thus would stop doing those things. His rationale was beguiling. "These concessions on the part of the 'enlightened' world will make it possible for us to achieve the unity and power that are needed in our struggle for national revival."

Grossman smiled. He said that as a founding father of Zionism, Ben-Yehuda needed to be seen now through a different prism. Embracing religion in the twenties was a way to fit into communal life. But religion wasn't an instrument among Zionists; on the contrary, it was seen as an obstacle. The Orthodox had in fact sought to sabotage as much as possible the overall ideological efforts of Zionism.

I told Grossman that part of my interest in Ben-Yehuda had to do with understanding how Hebrew had grown since 1948. Specifically, I was intrigued by the phenomenon of non-Jews learning Hebrew. "How many fundamentalist Christians know Hebrew?" I asked Grossman. "Judging by what I see in Jerusalem, as tourists they come in hordes. If the conditions are suitable, they visit the Christian sites and go back to their hotels. The industry must be good for Israel. For one thing, it brings revenue."

"They support Israel for a very simple reason," said Grossman. "They wouldn't want to see those sites in Muslim hands."

"They fear the return of Saladin to the Holy Land!" I exclaimed. "Yet it seems to me that fundamentalist Christians shouldn't be underestimated." I told Grossman that I had been looking into the work of Christian theologians, intellectuals, and academics in the United States, some of it dating back to the colonial period. For instance, William Bradford, a settler who came from Holland on the *Mayflower* and wrote a diary of his experiences as a leader of the first British colony, was a Hebraist. I explained that he and other Puritans identified with the myth of the Ten Lost Tribes of Israel. "It is clear from Bradford's *Of Plymouth Plantation* that he and his cohorts saw themselves as a generation in the wilderness, like the biblical Israelites. They had been expelled from England for their beliefs. They needed a safe haven, a Promised Land," I said.

"How much Hebrew did he know?" asked Grossman.

"That's a subject of debate," I replied. "But his passion

was endorsed over time by political figures such as Thomas Jefferson, who, in an 1812 exchange of correspondence with John Adams, insinuated that the Indian tribes on their side of the Atlantic Ocean might have descended from Jews, and that their language evolved from 'a common prototype,' biblical Hebrew." I told Grossman that the list of Hebraists in America was astonishing. "George Bush, an ancestor of presidents George H. W. and George W. Bush, was one. So were the explorer and consul Selah Merrill, the educational reformer William Rainey Harper, the theologian and pastor Reinhold Niebhur . . ."

How did Ben-Yehuda react to Hebrew being a language of non-Jews? Grossman believed it was a nonissue for him. "As long as the pioneers in Palestine learned it, as long as it was the nation's *only* tongue, the influential presence of Hebrew in Christian circles didn't bother him."

He was right. In *A Dream Come True*, Ben-Yehuda included a scene where he witnessed the Orientalist scholar and Hebrew writer Joseph Halévy in the classroom of a school run by the Alliance Israélite Universelle. Born in Adrianople, Turkey, Halévy moved to Paris, where he taught Ethiopian at the École Pratique des Hautes Études and was also a librarian at the Société Asiatique. He became an ardent Zionist and moved to Palestine to spread the gospel of Hebrew. The land was still under Ottoman rule. Ben-Yehuda described Halévy struggling to convey the importance of the language to Jewish students who appear too lazy to learn it and administrators who don't fully understand its value. Realizing how disappointing the effort was, Ben-

Yehuda heard a student say that "a Jew can be a good man without knowing Hebrew." He was appalled by Halévy's inability to respond. It seemed to him that the students had won the battle. Ben-Yehuda made it clear that in his mind you cannot have one without the other: Judaism *is* Hebrew.

Moving to another topic, Grossman expressed deep disappointment that Israeli literature is so little known in America. He stressed to me that his complaint wasn't primarily about book sales, or money. It struck him that American Jews were only marginally interested in what Israelis went through; they wanted to influence the course of events through lobbying or giving to Jewish philanthropies.

I asked Grossman if he thought this lack of interest had to do with American Jews for the most part not knowing Hebrew. Other than in Sunday school, the language is hardly taught in the United States. It's offered on a few college campuses, some of which offer only biblical Hebrew. But the number of registered students in modern Hebrew classes is infinitesimal compared to those studying popular languages such as Spanish and Chinese.

"Yes," said Grossman, and he added that for most people, Hebrew was the language of the Bible, not the language of Israel. The Hebrew heard on the evening news didn't appear to have anything to do with the story of Moses on Mount Sinai, King Solomon, and the prophets.

His comment made me think of Emma Lazarus, a canonical Jewish-American poet, whose poem "The New Colossus" appears on a plaque on the pedestal of the Statue of Liberty. Lazarus, who died in 1887, before the most significant events in Zionism of the late nineteenth century unfolded, was a translator into English of medieval Hebrew poets like Yehuda Halevi. But she accessed them tangentially. She seized on Hebrew as a literary—rather than a liturgical—language. Lazarus must have had some literacy in the language, having been raised near the Nineteenth Street Synagogue in New York City. But her Hebrew wasn't up to translating Halevi and other poets directly, so she used Abraham Geiger's German versions.

Eventually, Lazarus became frustrated and hired Louis Schnabel to be her Hebrew tutor. He inscribed to her a tiny book of Hebrew psalms, and she wrote Arabic numerals next to each Hebrew number. Lazarus begins the fourth installment of her *Epistle to the Hebrews*, written while she was studying Hebrew, with a paragraph on the "intensive voice." This becomes part of her claim that Jews are always the most intense form of any culture they inhabit. Before she died, not quite forty years old, Lazarus was able to translate a poem directly from Hebrew; it appeared in facsimile in *The American Hebrew*. This circuitousness is symbolic of the disconnection between American Jewish intellectuals and the Sacred Language.

Other people in the restaurant—waiters, chefs, patrons—kept coming over to talk to Grossman. He was clearly a celebrity. Strangers wanted to share with him an anecdote, to thank him for his courage. His response was customarily down-to-earth.

I told Grossman that in my readings of Christian thinkers I had come across Edmund Wilson, the author of *Axel's Castle* and *To the Finland Station*, who from his pulpit at *The New*

Yorker would be seen as America's literary deacon for two generations. "Wilson is an example of the non-Jewish Jew," I said. "In fact, after reading one of Wilson's articles in *Commentary*, John Dos Passos wrote to Wilson to say that he handled himself as 'an uncircumcised rabbi.' "

Grossman liked the image. He knew Wilson from his reportage on the Dead Sea Scrolls. "That's why Wilson taught himself Hebrew," I stressed. "He convinced the editor of *The New Yorker* to send him to Israel and Jordan, which he visited twice, his second trip being in 1967."

"Was he connected with Israel as a nation?" asked Grossman.

"He was attracted to it because of its biblical roots but mesmerized with Israel as a modern nation," I replied.

I mentioned reading an essay by Wilson titled "On First Reading Genesis," published in 1952, where he talks of his affair with the language of the Bible. "First of all, the surprises of the language," Wilson writes. "The Bible in Hebrew is far more a different thing than the Bible in any translation that the original Homer, say, is from the best of the translations of Homer, because the language in which it is written is more different from English than Greek is." He didn't think the King James Version did justice to the poetic nature of the original.

"In fact," I said, "Wilson believed that 'the Hebrew language is . . . emphatic to a degree with which our language can hardly compete.' " He argued:

The device for affirming something strongly is to repeat the important word, and God's warning to

Adam that he will "dying, die," if he disobeys His orders, seems weakened in [the King James] version—"thou shalt surely die"—as does Joseph's assertion that "stolen, I was stolen out of the land of the Hebrews" by "indeed I was stolen." Nor can we match the vehement expression of the violent Hebrew emotions. When Jehovah, about to invoke the Flood, has become disgusted with man, it is not adequate to say that the thoughts of man's heart were "only evil continually"; in the *"raq ra kol hayyóm"* of the text, we seem to hear the Creator actually spitting on his unworthy creation. . . . The violence and vehemence of Hebrew is implicit in the structure of the language itself. They did not conjugate their verbs for tenses, as the modern Western languages do, since our modern conception of time was something at which they had not yet arrived. . . . What the Hebrews had instead of tenses were two fundamental conjugations for perfect and imperfect—that is, for action completed and action uncompleted. And both of these two "aspects" theoretically exist in seven variations of every verb (though the complete set is rare) that have nothing to do with time.

I asked Grossman what he thought of the sentence "The violence and vehemence of Hebrew is implicit in the structure of the language itself."

He disagreed, stressing that there's no more violence in Hebrew than in any other Western language. And in this belief, too, Grossman may be a child of Ben-Yehuda, who strove to make Hebrew a daily tongue. For Wilson, Judeophile that he was, the Old Testament served as the depository of the language. For Grossman, as for Ben-Yehuda, Hebrew is a language like other languages—useful, neutral, and alive.

ע

On a breezy morning, I took a train to Hadera and from there to the Arab town of Baqa el Gharbiya (in Arabic, "the Western banquet"), seven and a half miles from the railway station. It was separated from the West Bank by a barrier built by Ariel Sharon's government; since then, its people have lived a divided existence. At one point, Sharon suggested he was ready to trade the town and other similar places in what is known as "the Arab triangle" for land used by the Jewish settlers.

I had heard about a grassroots effort in the Tel Aviv area in which elementary schools had recently introduced the teaching of the dialect of Palestinian spoken Arabic in the third grade and that some 65 percent of students in the city were involved in the program. Eager to corroborate these findings, I sought Dr. Faruq Mawasi, the vice president of the Writer's Union in Israel and one of a handful of Arabs who appeared to be active in Israeli institutions of higher learning. As the president of the Israeli branch of the Arabic Language Academy, Dr. Mawasi is among the world's specialists on Israeli Arabic. I wanted to know what his thoughts were on Eliezer Ben-Yehuda. I was curious about the strategies Palestinians and Arab Israelis use to communicate with one another, in particular Hirbia (aka Irvit), the hybrid spoken by approximately one million Arabs in Israel who mix Arabic and Hebrew in their daily communication.

Dr. Mawasi is in his mid-fifties. His spoken English is halting. (We spoke in a mixture of Arabic, Hebrew, and English.) Educated in Baqa el Gharbiya as well as in the village of Tayyiba, he received his undergraduate training in Israeli schools. He is proud of the doctorate he received from Tel Aviv University. (He wrote his doctoral dissertation on the Al-Diwan school of Arabic literature and its impact on English Romantic poetry.)

I told him that for years I had been interested in the mingling of Spanish and English, popularly known as Spanglish. This hybrid parlance is a by-product of diglossia—a social context where two closely related languages collide: one of them prestigious, endorsed by the government as well as educational and cultural institutions; the other considered unworthy and usually spoken as a vernacular. Spanglish is used by a wide array of speakers: young and old, rich and poor, male and female, coming from diverse national backgrounds from Puerto Rico to Argentina. Their way of communicating uses intriguing devices—code-switching, for instance. A Spanglish speaker might start a sentence in Spanish, then switch to English, going back and forth between the two languages. But the crossbreeding can be less apparent, allowing the syntax of one language to fertilize the other. Speakers might also engage in simultaneous translation, thinking in English but verbalizing in Spanish. Or they could use the thousands of Spanglish words they've coined over the years, which appear neither in the *Oxford English Dictionary* nor in the *Diccionario de la Lengua Española*. I suggested that this type of dialogue takes place because people live in two worlds. That is, their identities, American and Latino, are constantly overstepping each other.

Dr. Mawasi said that something similar takes place among Israeli Arabs. Whenever they travel to visit relatives in metropolises like Amman, Damascus, Beirut, Cairo, and Baghdad, they are ridiculed for their imperfect Arabic. Imperfection means contamination. The Hirbia they speak is a mishmash. It denotes acculturation. Rather than being perceived as objectors to Israel's colonialism, the response they receive is scorn: they are perceived as sellouts. Dr. Mawasi offered a few examples of cross-fertilization, which were identical in spirit to Spanglish. A sentence might begin in Arabic and move to Hebrew. Or there would be a plethora of Hebraisms sprinkling the dialogue. "Such linguistic practices are common. What are they to do?" he asked. "They live in two worlds. Those two worlds are represented by two languages. The two worlds are at war with each other. But unless governments impose undue restrictions, languages tend to contaminate each other."

By definition, language is imperfect. It will never capture the full range of our thoughts. Dr. Mawasi said that there was an added element to his description of Hirbia. "There's a tension between classical Arabic, which remains fossilized and isn't used on the street, and colloquial Arabic, which is spoken, in countless varieties, all over the Arab world." In recent years, he had cataloged a vast number of Hirbia terms, publishing them on his blog (geocities.com/faruq mawasi).

I asked Dr. Mawasi about the tension between classical Arabic and the language spoken by Israeli Arabs. He said that classical Arabic was the most popular Arabic language worldwide. One must keep in mind how large, in territorial terms, the Arab world is. Made up of twenty-three countries, it has a population of roughly 325 million people. The region extends from the Persian Gulf to the Indian Ocean, from Central Africa to the Mediterranean Sea. The Palestinian territories are a minuscule fraction of it, even though the news reports make people believe their presence is huge.

Arabic is closely related to Hebrew and Aramaic. There are a number of different colloquial Arabics but only one classical language, which has a normative approach, seeking to regulate the use of Arabic and to modulate its embrace of modernity. Writers use it, but, in wanting to reach as large an audience as possible, they often interject modern terms. Dr. Mawasi described for me the function of the Academy of the Arabic Language, whose foundation dates back to the early twentieth century, when nationalism spread in the Arab-speaking world. Its model was the Académie Française. The institution doesn't have a headquarters building for centralized control. Instead, each country has its own academy, the oldest of which is in Damascus. There are academies in Cairo, Amman, Khartum, and Rabat. The Damascus branch was created in 1918 under the reign of King

Faisal I, the branch in Cairo in 1934. A few years back an Arabic Academy was established in Israel. I asked if it had anything to do with the official Hebrew academy that had resulted from Eliezer Ben-Yehuda's efforts. "No," Dr. Mawasi said.

"Why is it that Israelis don't learn Arabic?" I inquired.

"They have no need for it," replied Dr. Mawasi. "They are the conquerors. They are the ones writing school textbooks." He was referring to the news items about the Israeli government deciding on the content of Arab textbooks used in Israeli schools. "Through those textbooks, they exercise control."

I switched the topic of conversation to Ben-Yehuda. In *A Dream Come True*, Ben-Yehuda showcased a desire to establish a partnership—political and cultural—with the Arabs in the land. This desire arose after Ben-Yehuda expressed a feeling of discomfort toward the Arabs in Palestine during Ottoman rule, a feeling that surprised him. "I was not prepared for this sensation," he wrote. In his eyes the land already had another identity. "Perhaps the dream that I had dreamt of a Jewish revival in the ancestral land really was nothing but a dream which had no place in reality." Although his discomfort was apparent, he nevertheless didn't delve into it. Instead, he looked for ways to interact with the Arabs in different spheres.

In reaction to the violence taking place in Palestine at the dawn of the twentieth century, at one point his son Itamar decided to write a letter (in French, one of Hemda's languages, which proves that his education wasn't so hermetic after all) to the Paris-based philanthropist Baron Edmond James de Rothschild. His purpose was clear: the formation of a unit designed to safeguard the Jewish settlers. The letter reads, in part:

Do not be surprised to receive this communication from your faithful servant.

The current events in some of the colonies of Your Excellency, at which a few farmers have been killed by their own so-called Arab guards, have caused great disturbance and excitement among the Jews of the country.

It is because of this that I, the undersigned, on behalf of my many friends, boys and girls (already a few hundred), appeal to Your Excellency with this proposition, daring, perhaps, at first sight.

I am ready to undertake the responsibility for the formation of the Hebrew army which will defend the colonies of Your Excellency.

This army, like the French Army, will be made of Jews and Arabs, the latter to be named *Légion Étrangère*.

As it is clear to me that such an army requires great funds, I propose to start small. One hundred men will be sufficient for the beginning, eighty Jews and twenty Arabs.

According to my estimate, it will be necessary to have one hundred pounds per month, in addition to the money required for uniforms and armament.

In order that Your Excellency will not support us of desiring the whole sum immediately, we shall appreciate it if we receive by the return of the mail the first one hundred napoleons for the purchase of uniforms for the officers.

We have already also started maneuvers. We also have already a flag which is herewith enclosed, along with my picture when I was four years old. The flag was drawn for us by David Ideolovitch from Rishon le-Zion, whom I call my uncle. This banner, as Your Excellency sees, is white, like the color of Israel in its white conscience.

Your Excellency will be pleased to hear that I have translated into Hebrew, for the purpose of a marching song, the first verse of the French *Marseillese* in abbreviation.

In older times we had Samsons, Maccabees, Bar-Kochbas. Why should we not today have "Rothschilds"?

Yes, Rothschilds, for this will be the name of our soldiers. Rothschilds with rifles and many napoleons, for, according to the Hebrew saying, "Money is the answer for everything."

Please, Your Excellency, answer with money and your name will be written in the history of Israel not only as our "Great Donor" but also as "Leader of the Army of Israel."

The letter was signed: Ben-Zion Ben-Yehuda, Colonel of the Hebrew Army.

What's amazing about this letter is that the boy asks that the Arabs be part of the army. This idea was no doubt discussed in the Ben-Yehuda household.

Dr. Mawasi didn't see my point; he viewed Ben-Yehuda as a colonialist forcing his culture on the aboriginal population of Palestine at the time.

"Ben-Yehuda included words with Arabic etymologies in his dictionary," I said. "Yet he excluded foreign words found even in the Bible, let alone the Talmud, and other works that aren't of Semitic origin."

"It's true," replied Dr. Mawasi, "but the gesture doesn't alleviate the pattern of abuse. Israelis have little patience for Arabic. They see it as an unworthy language. In school, they'll learn English, French, Russian, German. To learn Arabic they don't need to be in a classroom. It's alive on the street. But they are deaf."

Dr. Mawasi's view is understandable, given the relationship between Jews and Arabs in the country today. But it is nearsighted in that it ignores the spirit of collaboration that existed in the early stages of Zionism.

His reference to textbooks made me think of a watershed debate in Israeli culture between the Faulknerian Israeli novelist A. B. Yehoshua, author of classics like *A Late Divorce*, *Mr. Mani*, and *Open Heart*, and the Rothian Palestinian Christian Arab novelist Anton Shammas, author of *Arabesques*. Yehoshua had been an early supporter of Shammas and his book. Their debate took place after Shammas's book was published in 1986. It had been written in a gorgeous Hebrew with biblical resonances. Shammas's style was reminiscent of Agnon's, which isn't surprising since he studied at the Hebrew University. Shammas's sheer presence in the literary constellation made many in Israeli cultural circles believe that Hebrew was being deterritorialized.

In the debate, Shammas wanted to be seen as equal in Israel. He told Yehoshua, "Judaism also has to be separated from Israeliness."

Yehoshua responded negatively. "But how is that possible?" he said. "Try, for instance, separating France from Frenchness—is that possible?"

Shammas was prepared: "France and Frenchness come from the same stem, but Judaism and Israeliness is a different matter!" He added: "That's why I advocate the de-Judaization and de-Zionization of Israel."

Eventually, Yehoshua told Shammas that he couldn't have an Israeli identity because he was Palestinian. Shammas answered: "Yes, I am prepared to give up my Palestinian identity in the sense of a 'nation' as in a 'nation-state.' In other words, I am ready to give up being a national of the Palestinian State that will be established. I am prepared for my Palestinian identity to be an ethnic identity, the same as your Jewish identity."

Yehoshua laughed. "I don't need that folklorist ethnology."

Shammas eventually left Israel. (He now lives in Ann Arbor, Michigan.)

Dr. Mawasi took a dictionary from a nearby closet. Pointing to some definitions, he said the lexicographic effort of the Academies of the Arabic Language followed a strict scientific method. I asked him what he meant. "Entries are carefully calibrated," he replied. He talked of the *Al-Mu'jam Al-Kabir*, a dictionary that offers a comprehensive view of the history of the Arabic language; the *Al-Mu'jam Al-Wasit*, a lexicon of contemporary Arabic; and the *Al-Mu'jam Al-Wajiz*, a concise version for scholars.

They were made with the support of the Orientalist August Fisher.

He said that it was the duty of parents and teachers to educate their children in standard Arabic, to maintain the purity of their language. This statement struck me as conflicting with his research on Hirbia, and I told him so. "It's one thing to be attracted to the mishmash," he responded, "and another to promote it. Whenever I can, I correct Arabic-speaking parents in their misuse of the tongue. And I never tire of persuading Arab students that a clean language is proof of a healthy life."

פ

Another complex presence in Israel's verbal DNA is Yiddish.

Since the inception of the Jewish State, when the debate about language took place among its founding fathers (only a few women contributed to the shaping of Zionism as an ideology, among them Marie Syrkin; however, women in Mandate Palestine had the vote before they had it in the United States), *der mame-loshn* has sat uncomfortably on the horizon. The dream of creating a homeland was mounted on the premise that the Diaspora needed to come to an end. And Yiddish, more than any other language invented by the Jews, symbolized that Diaspora. That's apparently what Ben-Yehuda had carried out in his personal library: he expunged the Yiddish books. It is said that toward the end of his life, when he arrived in New York to work at the Public

Library on Forty-second Street and was greeted by Jewish children who welcomed him with songs, he covered his ears because they were singing in Yiddish and English.

I paid a visit to my old friend Chava Turniansky, who had been my Yiddish teacher in Mexico in the mid-eighties. She had been hired by a Jesuit university to give a series of lectures on Yiddish. I spent that semester as her student, delving into the work of Itzjok Leib Peretz, a magisterial Yiddish writer, intellectual, and editor with a unique approach to the Hasidic past. But she inspired me to read lesser-known, although not lesser-qualified, Yiddish authors, too, such as Lamed Shapiro, the first to ever write a pogrom story from the perspective of the assailant, and Pinhas Kahanovich ("Der Nister"), a Russian intellectual interested in Kabbalah who authored a genealogical novel, *The Family Mashber*, with mystical elements.

An emeritus professor at the Hebrew University in Jerusalem, Turniansky is a distinguished scholar who specializes in Yiddish literature and Ashkenazic culture in the early modern period. When we met, at a charming Mediterranean restaurant near Yaffo Street, Turniansky had just published a critical edition of the memoirs of Glückel of Hameln, an entrepreneurial Jewish woman in Germany in the late seventeenth and early eighteenth centuries who kept an insightful diary that serves as a window onto Jewish life before the Enlightenment. This critical edition became successful and brought Turniansky a wave of accolades.

With grim strokes, Turniansky described the situation of Yiddish in Israel. She said it was approached as a remnant of the past, ambivalently. At the university level, programs were poorly funded and students not committed to research, even though five students under Turniansky's advisorship had completed their PhDs in the year preceding my visit. It was the same picture others had drawn. If American Jews nurtured nostalgia toward Yiddish, that nostalgia existed only at the level of popular culture, in Hollywood movies and TV shows. It produced unlearned books targeting a general readership.

I told her that several days earlier Eliezer Nowodworski and I had been walking down a pleasant Tel Aviv boulevard when we noticed, hanging from the trees, posters promoting poetry as an integral part of urban life. They displayed "recreational" poems by Baudelaire, Paul Celan, and others, along with succinct biographical information. The effort looked like a preview of the city's approaching centennial festivities. The one poet representing Yiddish was Kadia Molodowski. Curiously, in just about every poster the original-language text was placed alongside the Hebrew translation. Molodowski—and, thus, Yiddish—was the only exception.

"There you have it, Ilan," Nowodworski had said to me. "Another perfect example of what I call 'the Holy Office of the Zionist Inquisition.' "

He was referring to the campaign by the founders of the State of Israel to erase all traces of Yiddish. The language, in their eyes, was a testimony to the miseries of the Diaspora. The only way to build the "new man" was to eradicate all traces of the old one.

When I mentioned the incident to Turniansky, she reminded me that Yiddish had originated in the Rhine region in the tenth century. The fact that Jews in the Pale of Settlement were polyglots is often seen as positive. We talked about a paper Max Weinreich had delivered at the Conference of Yiddish Studies in New York in 1958 in which he evaluated that quality. Later on, I found the piece, titled "Internal Bilingualism in Ashkenaz." In it Weinreich argued that the closeness of the languages (Hebrew and Yiddish) created many linguistic opportunities: phonetic integration, borrowing, calquing, purism, style, and stylization—all begging to be studied. As Weinreich says in his paper:

The learned men of Ashkenaz created neologisms like *mohel* "cirumciser" or *khalef* "slaughtering knife." With such redefinitions like *tseylem* from the Hebrew "image" to the Yiddish "crucifix," *bilbul*, from the Hebrew confusion to the Yiddish "false accusation," we are at the borderline between both languages, and that holds for the formation of expressions on the pattern of *meshane mokem meshane mazl*, "who changes his place changes his luck." But when we turn to the large categories of word formations like *baln balones*, or *baldarshn*, or *katsoves*, we are no longer on a borderline, but in a wide frontier belt with a condominium over both languages. In this shared linguistic territory, names like Hirsh, Wolf, Leyb, Ber, and the like were first translated into their Hebrew equivalents Zvi, Zev, Aryeh, Dov, and, thus, translated, they became elements in the Hebrew component of Yiddish.

Jews lived in the Polish-Lithuanian Commonwealth, the majority in shtetls, although a portion of the Jewish community made its home in Warsaw, Odessa, and Lublin. They spoke Polish, Lithuanian, Hungarian, Russian, and Czech, among other languages. Rabbinical discussion was read in the original Hebrew/Aramaic and discussed in Yiddish. Books in Hebrew and Yiddish were printed in Kraków and Lublin during the second half of the sixteenth century. Printing in these languages led to Haggadahs, prayer books, and dozens of other kinds of books and genres. Yiddish traveled from the oral to the written realm. The Talmud was first made available in Hebrew in 1484, thanks to the family-owned Soncino printers of Lombardy. But access to these Hebrew and Aramaic books was limited to the educated elite. Elijah Levita's *Bove Bukh* was intended for women, but because of its appeal, it was read by men, too; the anonymous *Tsene-rene* was intended for men and women alike but became the most popular book for women. Glückel of Hameln wrote her memoirs for her children, both boys and girls. Only the *tkhines*, Yiddish-language prayer books, were written exclusively for women.

"The promiscuity of Yiddish and Hebrew is at the core of Ashkenazic civilization," said Turniansky. This is especially obvious among nineteenth-century *mitnagdim*, educators and intellectuals whose mission was to embrace the ideas of the Enlightenment. "Think of Mendele Mokher Sforim," said

Turiansky, referring to the so-called grandfather of Yiddish literature. An educator and writer responsible for *Fishke the Lame*, considered to be the first serious novelistic effort among Yiddish writers, he was born in 1836 and died in 1917. "Mendele was fluent in Hebrew and Yiddish, among other languages," said Turniansky. "When he decided to write a novel, his choice and decision as a committed *maskil* was to do it in Hebrew, considered to be the educated tongue. But he wanted to reach the masses, and so he was tempted by Yiddish. In his autobiography, *Reshimot Le-Toldotay* [*Notes About My Life*], he said that he tried to compose a story in simple Hebrew, grounded in the spirit and life of the Jewish people at the time, a life that was lived mainly in Yiddish. But he faced a wall. His thinking was: 'Observing how my people lived, I want to write stories for them in our sacred tongue, yet most do not understand the language. They speak Yiddish. What good is the writer's work if people won't read him?' In Mendele's time, Yiddish was looked down upon by the intellectual elite as a nonsense language used only by women, children, and the illiterate."

By the dawn of the twentieth century, Yiddish was the quintessential expression of the Ashkenazic psyche. As proof of its importance, Turniansky made reference to the translations into Yiddish of Shakespeare, Cervantes, and Spinoza. Publishing houses brought out novels, plays, essays, and nonfiction. At the widely publicized Czernowitz Conference in Bukovina of August 1908, the scholar Ba'al Makshoves said that Jewish literature, from its inception, had nearly always been bilingual. He argued that bilingualism is such an old ailment among Jews that it long ago ceased to pose a threat to the Jewish organism.

Zionists like Eliezer Ben-Yehuda, however, didn't want to get lost in a labyrinth. The only way to build a state was through a single tongue. And determination was needed to choose Hebrew over Yiddish. The approach wasn't lopsided, of course. A devotion to Yiddish could be sensed at the top of the Zionist political ladder. For instance, Levi Eshkol (born Levi Shkolnik near Kiev, in the Ukraine), elected to the Knesset in 1951 and Israel's third prime minister, was famous for his Yiddishisms.

"What about Yitzhok Bashevis Singer?" asked Turniansky. "You've collected his stories in English, Ilan." She used the Yiddishized appellation of Isaac Bashevis Singer, arguably the most polarizing person ever connected with Yiddish letters. (He has been called "Mendele's bastard.") Singer was born in Poland in 1904 and died in Florida in 1991. His life journey was a register of the principal challenges *der mame-loshn* faced in the twentieth century. His 1978 Nobel Prize for Literature authenticated his role in the Western world, but among Yiddishists he was anathema. They saw him as a usurper and a charlatan who, through his fiction, injected an anachronistic dose of eroticism into the shtetl.

When Singer arrived in New York City, at the age of thirty-one, he became disheartened by the way Yiddish was spoken by immigrants in America. It was no longer the coherent language he had used in Warsaw, where he published his first novel, *Satan in Goray*. It was a disgusting concoction. What he heard wasn't Yiddish, nor was it English; it was Yinglish. By the time he received the Nobel Prize, his critics were to argue that he himself was a Yinglish master. Still, in his Stockholm address, he portrayed Yiddish as eternal:

> To me the Yiddish language and the conduct of those who spoke it are identical. One can find in the Yiddish tongue and in the Yiddish style expressions of pious joy, lust for life, longing for the Messiah, patience, and deep appreciation of human individuality. There is a quiet humor in Yiddish and a gratitude for every day of life, every crumb of success, each encounter of love. The Yiddish mentality is not haughty. It does not take victory for granted. It does not demand and command but it muddles through, sneaks by, smuggles itself amid the powers of destruction, knowing that God's plan for creation is still at the very beginning.
>
> There are some who call Yiddish a dead language, but so was Hebrew called for two thousand years. It has been revived in our time in a most remarkable, almost miraculous way. Aramaic was certainly a dead language for centuries, but then it brought to light the *Zohar*, a work of mysticism of sublime value. It is a fact that the classics of Yiddish literature are also the classics of the modern Hebrew literature. Yiddish has not yet said its last word. It contains treasures that have not been revealed to the eyes of the world. It was the tongue of martyrs and saints, of dreamers and Kabbalists—rich in humor and in memories that mankind may never forget. In a fugitive

way, Yiddish is the wise and humble language of us all, the idiom of frightened and hopeful humanity.

Singer visited Israel a number of times. His only son (from his first wife, Runya), Israel Zamir, was a kibbutznik. The son and his mother didn't go to the United States with Singer. He left them behind. They eventually went to Russia, then traveled to Israel via Turkey. After years of not being in touch, Zamir came to New York and knocked at the door of his illustrious father. The response he got was cold at first. Eventually they made peace, and the son became his father's Hebrew translator. Hebrew translations of Singer's works had appeared in Israel (the first in 1953) long before Israel Zamir started translating them.

I wondered if in some people's eyes it was an affront to the idea of Israel for a writer like Singer to receive the Nobel Prize.

"It may be that there is still an element of distaste for him," Turiansky said.

I told Turniansky I had just visited Beit Sholem Aleichem in downtown Tel Aviv. Her smile made it clear to me that the place needed to be approached with caution.

The institution, a precious piece of real estate located at 4 Berkowitz Street, in a fancy neighborhood of tall buildings (the Israeli equivalent of skyscrapers) that stand erect as emblems of a thriving economy, is not too far from the courthouse and the Performing Arts Center. I was greeted by Nowodworski's mother, Esther Rollansky, who teaches there. She gave me a tour. Yiddish courses and lectures are offered on a regular basis, as well as yearlong seminars on Jewish civilization in Eastern Europe. The problem, it seems, is that students aren't granted credit for these studies in any university. They go to study Yiddish in institutions such as the Hebrew University, Bar-Ilan University, and universities in Beer-Sheva and Haifa. In a society geared toward practicalities, this is a huge obstacle.

The truth is, Sholem Aleichem *was* a Zionist, although his views on the Jewish State were complex. In 1898, he published an essay called "Why Do Jews Need a Land of Their Own?" He attended every Zionist Congress, gave public readings on behalf of the cause, and was a member of Chovevei Zion, a proto-Zionist group, but his fictional characters, when faced with a choice of where to immigrate, mostly bypass Israel. Sholem Aleichem lived in Odessa and Kiev, among other places. Trying to make a living in Yiddish theater, he immigrated to New York City in 1906, when he was forty-seven; he left after a couple of years and came back in 1914, just before World War I broke out. He died two years later, at the age of fifty-seven, and is buried at the Mount Carmel Cemetery in Queens. Eighty years later, a stretch of East Thirty-third Street between Park and Madison Avenues, where the offices of the *Jewish Daily Forward* are located, was renamed Sholem Aleichem Place. It's one of very few official sites paying tribute to him; others include a monument that an anti-Semitic politician erected in Kiev in 1997, in order to attract foreign investors to the city, and one erected in Moscow in 2001. His connection to the State of Israel was solidified by his son-in-law, Itzjok Dov Berkovicz, after whom the street on which Beit Sholem Aleichem is located is named; Berkovicz bought the piece of real estate. He made every effort to preserve his father-in-law's oeuvre, starting with the translations he did of Sholem Aleichem's works from Yiddish into Hebrew.

Berkovicz's support wasn't disinterested. When World War I broke out, he was in the United States, where he lived until 1928, at which time he moved to Tel Aviv. He censored the Hebrew renditions he made of Sholem Aleichem, simplifying his father-in-law's complex views on Israel. He transformed one of the most renowned characters, Menachem Mendl, from the epistolary novel *Menachem Mendl*, into an outspoken Zionist and wrote a play of his own, *Menachem Mendl in Eretz Isroel*, in which the protagonist writes letters about how glorious the Promised Land is.

Mostly what I saw on display at Beit Sholem Aleichem were artifacts from Sholem Aleichem's life in an exhibition that included phylacteries, passports, and editions of his works in a variety of languages. As I browsed through them, I experienced a sense of uneasiness. The museum didn't feel right. It was a tribute to arguably the best Jewish writer ever—or at least the most popular. But Israel wasn't a suitable place for him. His presence felt parenthetical.

צ

In Steimatzky, the Israeli bookstore chain, a branch of which one finds in every commercial district, I bought myself a copy of the Hebrew translation of Jorge Luis Borges's book *The Aleph and Other Stories*.

The purchase wasn't accidental. In more ways than one, my search for Eliezer Ben-Yehuda's path was a reflection of my own journey, and the Argentine master, although a non-Jew, had helped me, at different moments, to figure out my own relationship with Israel.

A Judeophile with a penchant for the supernatural, Borges, in April 1934, at the age of thirty-five, wrote a brief essay called "I, a Jew." He published it in the Buenos Aires magazine *Megáfono* in response to accusations from another periodical, the conservative *Crisol*, that he was Jewish. In the piece, Borges argued that throughout his life he had been unsuccessful in finding the Jewish link that would make him happy.

I am grateful for the stimulus provided by *Crisol*, but hope is dimming that I will ever be able to discover my link to the Table of the Bread and the Sea of Bronze; to Heine, Gleizer, and the ten *Sefiroth;* to Ecclesiastes and Chaplin.

Statistically, the Hebrews were few. What would we think of someone in the year 4000 who uncovers people from San Juan Province everywhere? Our inquisitors seek out Hebrews, but never Phoenicians, Garamantes, Scythians, Babylonians, Persians, Egyptians, Huns, Vandals, Ostrogoths, Ethiopians, Illyrians, Paphlagonians, Sarmatians, Medes, Ottomans, Berbers, Britons, Libyans, Cyclopes, or Lapiths. The nights of Alexan-

dria, of Babylon, of Carthage, of Memphis, never succeeded in engendering a single grandfather; it was only
to the tribes of the bituminous Dead Sea that this gift
was granted.

It might have been that empathy that made him produce
an oeuvre populated by Jewish characters and with Jewish
concerns: Jaromir Hladik in "The Secret Miracle," the need
to question God in "Emma Zunz," the Tetragramaton used
as a detective clue in "Death and the Compass." Borges visited Israel on two occasions: in 1969, when he lectured in
Jerusalem and Tel Aviv, and in 1971, to receive the Jerusalem
Prize. During the Six-Day War he was an unequivocal supporter of the young nation, publishing two poems, one of
them a sonnet celebrating its victory against its Arab enemies, the other calling Hebrew "a tongue that praises from
the depths / the justice of the skies." Yet Borges's connection with Zionism wasn't without complications. He questioned the need to create a Jewish State when the Jews in the
Diaspora had excelled as outsiders. Why make them insid-
ers? he wondered. Why the need to normalize their existence? To the Zionist, the answer is obvious: because in
addition to growing tired of being killed, they were tired of
fulfilling other people's outsider fantasies.

As much as I admire Borges's oeuvre, I'm conscious of its
ahistoricism. It's one thing for pre-Holocaust intellectuals
to think that aside from a handful of inconvenient anti-
Semitic outbursts the Diaspora could be perceived as a bliss-
ful state, but it's altogether different, in the second half of

the twentieth century, to look at Israel as an anachronism. There's something sentimental, nostalgic, and downright naive in Borges's views on Israel. After 1948, the idea of the Jew as an outsider can no longer be approached without profound skepticism. This doesn't mean, in my view, that the Diaspora as an option has disappeared. It simply has been reconsidered from a less passive, more complex perspective.

That afternoon, after returning to my hotel, I read from beginning to end the Hebrew paperback copy of *The Aleph* I had acquired. Translated by Yoram Bronovsky, its style is succinct, mathematical. (It comes with almost twenty pages of notes.) The story I was most interested in was "The Aleph" itself. Borges chose the word *aleph*, the first letter of the Hebrew alphabet, with its numeric value 1, as the title of the story he published in Buenos Aires, in Victoria Ocampo's magazine *Sur*, in September 1945 (and in collected form in 1949). At its center is an object at once ordinary and mysterious. Borges modeled his narrative after the *Divine Comedy*, making the protagonist a seeker in search of an inner vision. His idealized love, Beatriz Viterbo, has just died; in longing for her, he visits the house of Viterbo's cousin, Carlos Argentino Daneri, who in turn introduces him to "a magic artifact placed in the cellar, barely wider than the staircase" the narrator uses to descend, "more like a well or cistern."

The vision Borges's protagonist receives is incredible. He comes across a sphere approximately an inch in diameter, but "universal space was contained inside it, with no diminution in size." At first, it appears to him to be spinning, but the movement is an illusion. "Each thing (the glass surface of a mirror, let us say) was infinite things, because I could clearly see it from every point of the cosmos." An entire page in the story is devoted to what the protagonist sees. In Andrew Hurley's English rendition:

> I saw the populous sea, saw dawn and dusk, saw the multitudes of the Americas, saw the silvery spider-web at the center of a black pyramid, saw a broken labyrinth (it was London), saw endless eyes, all very close, studying themselves in me as though in a mirror, saw all the mirrors on the planet (and none of them reflecting me), saw in a rear courtyard on Calle Soler the same tiles I had seen twenty years before in the entryway of a house in Fray Bentos, saw clusters of grapes, snow, tobacco, veins of metal, water vapor, saw convex equatorial deserts and their every grain of salt, saw a woman in Inverness whom I shall never forget, saw her violent hair, her haughty body, saw a cancer in her breast, saw a circle of dry soil within a sidewalk where there had once been a tree, saw a country house in Adrogué, saw a copy of the first English translation of Pliny (Philemon Holland's), saw every letter of every page at once (as a boy, I would be astounded that the letters in a closed book didn't get scrambled up together overnight), saw simultaneous night and day, saw a sunset in Querétaro that seemed to reflect the color of a rose in Bengal, saw my bedroom (with no one in it), saw in a study in Alkmaar a globe of the earthly

world placed between two mirrors that multiplied it endlessly, saw horses with wind-whipped manes on a beach in the Caspian Sea at dawn, saw the delicate bones of a hand, saw the survivors of a battle sending postcards, saw a Tarot card in a shop window in Mirzapur, saw the oblique shadows of ferns on the floor of a greenhouse, saw tigers, pythons, bison, tides, and armies, saw all the ants on earth, saw a Persian astrolabe, saw in a desk drawer (and the handwriting made me tremble) obscene, incredible, detailed letters that Beatriz had sent Carlos Argentino, saw a beloved monument in Chacarita, saw the horrendous remains of what had once, deliciously, been Beatriz Viterbo, saw the circulation of my dark blood, saw the coils and springs of love and the altercations of death, saw the Aleph from everywhere at once, saw the earth in the Aleph, and the Aleph once more in the earth and the earth in the Aleph, saw my face and my viscera, saw your face . . .

In an interview he gave in his mature years, Borges explained his choice of the first Hebrew letter by pointing to his interest in *lo judío*, things Jewish, particularly to the kabbalistic tradition of the *Sefiroth*. He said that in that tradition the letter had magical powers capable of bridging the personal and universal realms. Fittingly, "The Aleph" contains an epigraph from Shakespeare's *Hamlet*, Act II, Scene 2: "O God, I could be found in a nutshell and count myself a King of infinite space." At the end of the story, as Borges's protagonist receives his vision, he suddenly becomes dizzy. Borges writes: "And I wept, because my eyes had seen that secret, hypothetical object whose name has been usurped by men but which no man has ever truly looked upon: the inconceivable universe."

I felt moved while remembering my teacher at the Yidishe Shule saying to me that in Hebrew my name starts with an *aleph*.

A few days earlier I had spent some time with Rabbi Rebecca Krausz. We had met in the mid-eighties at the Jewish Theological Seminary when I delivered a series of lectures on Borges. Originally from Paris, Rabbi Krausz is the daughter of Holocaust survivors.

In her late forties, Rabbi Krausz looks like the actress Helena Bonham-Carter. She had invited me to attend a talk on Abraham Abulafia's *Sefer ha-Ot* (*Book of the Sign*) and on his commentaries on the canonical book *Sefer Yetzirah* (*Book of Creation*). Abulafia was a thinker from Saragossa who believed that through *gematria*, a system of using the numerical value of the Hebrew alphabet to extract meaning from biblical passages, as well as through ritual, a devout Jew might be able to attain the highest level of existence—that is, to become a prophet. His theory wasn't designed to make Isaiahs out of all of us but to inspire people to sharpen their perceptive and intellectual qualities, to make them more prone to decipher the deeper meanings of God's creation.

After the lecture, Rabbi Krausz and I shared some tapas at a restaurant near the Hotel Dan Panorama. I asked her why the *aleph* was the first letter in the alphabet. She told me that among the Phoenicians, an agricultural civilization, the same letter also came first. It was represented by an ox head, epitomizing strength, power, and leadership. The ox came to symbolize cattle. As the letter traversed history, it represented a prince and a champion. Its ancient name was *al*. Among the Phoenicians, a civilization of marine navigators, the letter was a glottal stop. The Phoenician graph morphed into the Hebrew א (*aleph*). Then the Phoenicians traveled to Greece, influencing arts and politics. (In *Histories* V, Herodotus refers to the Phoenician alphabet as *phoinikeia grammata*.) The letter mutated into α, called *alpha*. "The *aleph* comes first not only for the Phoenicians but in every Semitic language, dating back to at least 1300 B.C.E.," said Rabbi Krausz.

On a napkin, she drew a bird:

"The image isn't fully accurate but should do the trick," she said. "In Egyptian hieroglyphics, the *aleph* is represented by a bird." She went on to say that in Arabic the name of the letter is *alif*, and subsequently, in the Roman alphabet as well as in Cyrillic, the *aleph* became the upper-case *A* and lower-case *a*.

Rabbi Krausz paused, then added: "The bird might be seen as the ancestor of your imaginary bird."

I didn't understand the reference.

"The *Liwerant*," she continued, "the imaginary creature you wrote me about years ago."

"I did?"

"Sure," responded Rabbi Krausz. "It was part woman, part feathered vertebrate with forelimbs modified to form wings."

I was enthralled by the reference to the *Liwerant*, the creature in my dream that nobody I knew recognized. I told her about the dream I had had that prompted me to embark on my search for the history of the Hebrew language. I mentioned the attractive woman talking about the imaginary bird. I said that I had been hunting for a clue to its provenance. How could it be that I didn't have any recollection of mentioning it to Rabbi Krausz?

"Unbelievable, Ilan. Years ago, you sent me a newspaper clipping in which you described the bird in full."

A vague memory suddenly began to come back. In the late eighties I wrote a column for newspapers such as *El Diario/La Prensa* in New York. I might have written a piece about a fabulous beast with similar characteristics to the bird Rabbi Krausz and I were discussing.

"Look it up! You'll see that I'm right."

Attempting to hide my embarrassment, I pursued the topic of the *aleph*.

"But why does *aleph* come first?" I wondered. "Why not *gimmel*? Or *tav*? Or *yud*?"

"Ah, the question is at the core of Jewish theology," she replied. "The *aleph* isn't the opening letter in the Torah. Genesis 1:1 starts with *bet*."

"Why?"

"Its shape makes it look like a right-through entrance. Thus, it symbolizes the beginning." She paused. "In compensation, *aleph* comes first in Exodus 20:2, which showcases the Decalogue: I am the Lord thy God. It is also the first letter of the words *Adam* and *Abraham*."

Rabbi Krausz's comments echoed the kabbalistic wisdom that the privilege a letter enjoys of opening a significant word—first is best—elevates its stature. "The Hebrew word for 'oxygen' starts with *aleph*, as do those for 'happiness' and 'luck.' And, as with *H* in the Roman alphabet, *aleph* is silent although not mute, acquiring different phonetic sounds according to its position." Rabbi Krausz added, "In the Talmud, *aleph* denotes unity: one God, one Israel, one Torah . . . oneness as a synonym of uniqueness."

Rabbi Krausz's disquisition left me bewildered. I pursued the track of the letter and found that according to *Sefer ha-Zohar*, *aleph* symbolizes the divine energy needed by the Almighty for the creation of the universe. For that reason, it represents a readiness to act, whereas the second letter, *bet*, represents action itself. Rabbi Akiva (ca. 95–135 C.E.) believed that the Hebrew letters were hidden for two thousand years prior to the creation of the world. Just as God was about to start the act of creation, all twenty-two appeared before Him. The letter *tav*, the twenty-second, said, "Oh Lord, create the world through me, for I am the beginning of the word *Torah*."

Rabbi Krausz added that in the Jewish imagination *aleph* represents the totality of things, which makes it the most important letter. "It doesn't take away from its relevance that the letter is stunningly elegant to the eye, a badge intersected by a leg on the bottom left and an arm on the upper right. Among rabbis after the destruction of the Second Temple, it was construed to be 'the primary source.' "

Back in my hotel, I read Bronovsky's translation of "The Aleph" with enormous attention. Borges's story felt primal in Hebrew, as if the translation had made it travel closer to its source. Somehow, reading it in Israel made me sensitive to its Jewishness.

I would continue to be haunted by the mystery of the order of the letters in the Hebrew alphabet. Months later, a friend directed me to the following midrash, included in Howard Schwartz's anthology *Tree of Souls:*

God replied, "*Tav,* You are worthy and deserving, and in days to come I shall command that you be put as a sign on the foreheads of the righteous, so that when the destroyed angel comes to punish sinners, he will see the letter on their foreheads and spare them." But the letter *tav* was sad that it would not be used to create the world, and it left the presence of the Lord.

Then, one by one, each of the other letters came forward and pleaded with God to create the world through them. But God did not grant their wish. Soon all that remained were two letters, *aleph* and *bet. Bet* came forth and said, "Oh Lord, it would be appropriate to create the world through me, for your children will praise you through me every time they say "Blessed be the Lord for ever and ever."

Then God said, "Blessed are you who come in the name of the Lord." And God took the letter *bet* and created the world through it.

All this time the letter *aleph* had stood silent. Then God called it and said, "Why are you silent?" *Aleph* replied, "Master of the universe, I am the least among the letters, for my value is for one. How can I presume to approach you?"

The words of the letter *aleph* were pleasing to God, and He said, "Because you are so modest, you shall become the foremost among the letters, for just as your value is one, so am I one and the Torah is one."

Louis Ginzberg, the Lithuanian Talmudist who was responsible for the multivolume *Legends of the Jews*, offers a longer, more detailed version of the same midrash. In it God is about to create the world. The twenty-two letters of the alphabet descended from the terrible and august crown of God, whereon they were engraved with a pen of flaming fire. They stood around God, and one after the other spoke and entreated, "Create the world through me!" The first to step forward was the letter *tav*. It said to God: "O Lord of the word! May it be Thy will to create Thy world through me, seeing that it is through me that thou wilt give the Torah to Israel by the hand of Moses, as it is written: 'Moses commanded us the Torah.' " The Holy One, blessed be He, made a reply, and said, "No!" *Tav* asked, "Why not?" and God answered: "Because in days to come I shall place thee as a sign of death upon the foreheads of men."

Slowly, as each of the letters approached God, they were given an explanation of what their role in nature would be. Then the letter *bet* stepped forward and said: "Oh Lord of the world! May it be Thy will to create Thy world through me, seeing that all the dwellers in the world give praise daily unto Thee through me, as it is said, 'Blessed be the Lord forever. Amen and Amen.' " Granting the petition, God said: "Blessed be he that cometh in the name of the Lord. *Bereshit* God created the heaven and the earth." The midrash concludes by stating that the only letter that had refrained from urging its claims was *aleph*, and God later rewarded it for its humility by giving it the first place in the Decalogue.

I thought to myself that probably no other Hebrew letter has been more inspiring. The first few lines of Samuel Taylor Coleridge's poem "Kubla Khan: or, A Vision in a Dream," written in the British farmhouse of Exmoor in 1797 or 1798 and published in 1816, came to my mind:

> In Xanadu did Kubla Khan
> a stately pleasure-dome decree:
> where Alph, the secret river, ran
> through caverns measureless to man
> down to the sunless sea.

Why would Coleridge choose to name an ancestral current with the first Hebrew letter? As I reread "The Aleph" in Hebrew in my Tel Aviv hotel, it dawned on me that Israel itself was a sort of Borgesian *aleph*. All things Jewish were conflated in it. The nation was a sum of Diasporic parts, a site where the universe entire is contained.

ק

Upon returning home after one of my trips to Israel, I looked in my archives for clippings of the newspaper column to see if I had indeed written about the *Liwerant*. The place where I do most of my writing is a large rectangular room on the third floor of the Dutch Colonial house where I live in Amherst, Massachusetts. Next to it there is a closet (I call it my *genizah*) where I store my papers. After about half an hour I found the clipping.

"Unbelievable indeed," I thought. "I've been after an explanation of the image in my dream, constantly asking people about it, when I myself have had the clue to solve the enigma all along."

In 1989, I wrote in Spanish about a dream I had had—was it the first of its kind? I now wonder—in which I saw the *Liwerant*. I translate a segment here:

The Sphinx, called Androsphinx by Herodotus, is a lion with the head of a human. The *Liwerant* isn't a hybrid. It is shaped like a *guajolote*, with a long beak that has a carbuncle hanging under it. From a distance its minuscule head makes it look as if it had been decapitated. The legs end in three claws. It cannot fly. There is something trenchant in its eyes that the poet Ollin Yolitzi described as "menacing, like a cobra."

The only mention of it is in *Nahuatl Miscellany* (1687), by Fray Joaquín Santiago de Benavente.

The provenance of the *Liwerant* is in question. It has never been seen in Europe. In the Americas it has been spotted only twice: once in the Isthmus of Tehuantepec, on the Oaxacan coast; the other time in Peru, in the Ballestas Islands.

I felt cheated. Still, after rereading the text I foolishly went to the library in search of *Nahuatl Miscellany.*

It was a hoax, of course; I had invented it.

I had become a victim of my own tricks. I had now dreamed about the *Liwerant* twice. What was its role in my second dream, the one with the naked woman? Maybe to signify that language is also an imaginary creation. Where do words come from? Not from the world itself, for sure. The word *automobile* has nothing to do with the automobile as an object. It's a man-made concoction. And why do we employ it to describe the self-propelled passenger vehicle that generally has four wheels and an internal-combustion engine, used for land transport? Why not refer to it as *sugar*? Or with a nonsensical word like *kraspurgis*?

There was another aspect of the dream that I now more than ever wanted to sort out. In my dream the *Liwerant* supposedly sang to the rhythm of some peculiar tunes. And it ate *yarmelaki*. What's a *yarmelaki*?

I next saw Rabbi Krausz a few months later in Berlin. She had moved there with her husband, Ernest Klingman, whose Internet business had been relocated there. They invited me to their home for dinner.

I told them about finding the newspaper clipping in my

genizah, that memory had played tricks on me. Indisputably I knew what the *Liwerant* was, for I had created the creature from my own imagination.

Both laughed.

"By the way, do you know what a *yarmelaki* is?" I asked.

They looked at me in astonishment. After a moment of silence, Rabbi Krausz said: "I don't know. Could it be related to the Yiddish word *yarmulke*? If so, maybe it's a reference that associated the Hebrew language with its religious foundation. Might it be that you invented it as well?"

"Perhaps," I replied.

"I can't figure out the etymology of the name," she said. "It sounds Greek. Maybe it's the first word of some story, as in the Torah. The book of Genesis is called *Bereshit* after its first word." She paused. "Or it can happen that you'll never know."

Rabbi Krausz said that a few months earlier she and Ernest had gone to London's National Gallery, where they had seen Rembrandt's painting *Belshazzar's Feast*.

I told her I had also been to the National Gallery to see it.

"Rembrandt included in Hebrew letters a quote, which he painted in yellow in an illuminated circle in the upper right corner of the painting: *Mene, Mene Tekel Upharsin.*"

"What does it mean?" I asked.

"It's the 'writing on the wall' from Daniel 5:25. The passage—in Aramaic—that the king of Babylon, Belshazzar, son of Nebuchadnezzar, utters to a gathering of wise men in Babylon while offering wine in vessels his troops looted from the destroyed Temple in Jerusalem." She paused. "Rembrandt writes it vertically, not horizontally. Nobody is clear why."

"He could have written *yarmelaki* instead," Ernest remarked. "Don't you think? How frightening! Imagine one day visiting the National Gallery and, while looking at a painting, realizing one of the faces in it is yours?"

I liked the idea but felt uncomfortable and didn't know what to say.

Over dessert, the discussion turned to the friendship between Gershom Scholem and Walter Benjamin. In Rabbi Krausz's view, it was a perfect example of "the longing for Eretz Yisrael that has Hebrew as its conduit." Sholem and Benjamin became close friends from the moment they met in Berlin. Scholem was a Zionist interested in the Jewish mystical tradition. When he made aliyah, he was hired to teach at the Hebrew University. In a memoir of his youth called *From Berlin to Jerusalem*, published in 1977, Scholem wrote about learning Hebrew and being ashamed of his German accent in it at a time when most immigrants in Palestine were from Russia. "From the beginning I made hardly any mistakes in writing the languages that I learned," wrote Scholem, "for I could visualize the words written in front of me. My acoustical memory, on the other hand, did not amount to much. Then, too, I saw little reason to exchange my Hebrew as shaped by the Berlin cadences for the Russian accent, which was obviously just as incorrect. If anyone had spoken with a Semitic accent, influenced by Arabic—as did, for example, Oriental Jews—I would probably have made a greater effort in that direction."

Rabbi Krausz said that Scholem began to publish in

Hebrew when he was around twenty-seven years old. It wasn't easy. Even though he had had intensive instruction in Hebrew, he still was a long way from the free association that makes fruitful and effective expression possible. She said that, according to Scholem, the number of German Jews of his generation who became successful Hebrew speakers remained low. He perceived himself as one of the lucky few.

But Benjamin, an unorthodox Marxist, wasn't as lucky. "The world entire was a text for him," said Rabbi Krausz. "Fingerprints, Mickey Mouse, a corpse, daguerreotypes, Kafka, the Paris arcades, Baudelaire, book collecting." As darkness was overtaking Europe, Scholem tried to convince Benjamin that Israel would be a suitable place for him to continue his intellectual endeavors. It seems that Benjamin did take his friend's suggestion to heart. But in order for the aliyah to happen, he needed to learn Hebrew first. He talked about it with others. And he tried—unsuccessfully. Since his unorthodox cultural criticism was looked down upon in the German academic environment, he needed to support himself by freelancing. Rabbi Krausz mentioned a letter that Benjamin wrote to his friend Hugo von Hofmannsthal. I looked it up later. It's dated March 17, 1928:

I now seize the opportunity to tell you something about my innermost intentions, and to speak about external matters that seem to be taking shape more quickly than I had imagined. In short, the University of Jerusalem intends to add an Institute for the Humanities in the near future. And I must say that they have in mind to appoint me professor of modern German and French literature. The one condition is that I acquire a solid command of Hebrew in two to three years. This should not be understood as implicitly intended to fix my area of specialization. Instead, the goal is to introduce me to things Jewish in a very organic way and to leave the degree to which this occurs completely open. As for me, I find myself being able to speak of the rare case in which my desires, which in this form were still almost unconscious, were identified for me from one perspective. Nothing would intrinsically appeal to me more than initially to deal as a learner with only one problem of language, that is, with the technical problem, protectively surrounded by my former projects, and to leave everything else in abeyance.

"Benjamin's quest for Hebrew is like Kafka's infatuation with Yiddish: it was a Platonic love affair without practical consequences," announced Rabbi Krausz.

I hadn't thought of learning a language (or not) as a way to survive. She added: "It's as if German were at war with Hebrew."

Soon I realized that talking about Hebrew in Germany made me uncomfortable. I told her about an experience I had had years ago in Prague, at the tomb of the Maharal, Rabbi Judah Loew, the creator of the Golem. His tombstone in the Old Jewish Cemetery is covered with candle wax and scribbled notes are inserted in the crevices. These notes are written by pilgrims asking him for protection or maybe a miracle to be performed on their behalf. I wanted to write a note myself. Since I hadn't brought any blank paper, I used the back of a business card and wrote on it a message to God. Three months later, back at home, I got a letter from a German youngster. While traveling in Prague, his school had visited the Old Jewish Cemetery and stopped at the Maharal's tomb, where he stumbled upon my note. He apologized for the intrusion, yet he wanted me to explain to him my need to communicate with God.

I had felt offended.

"Why?" asked Rabbi Krausz.

"A German had yet again interfered in a Jew's attempt to talk to his God."

"What did you do?" she asked.

"I wrote him back. It wasn't an angry letter. In the end I said he wasn't to be blamed for his curiosity. It was History, with a capital *H*, the one that made us enemies. But we didn't have to follow the script if we chose not to."

She paused. "In what language did you write to God?"

A heavy silence fell over me. "Mmm . . . I don't remember."

"In English?" Ernest inquired.

"It couldn't have been in Spanish, because I doubt the youngster would have understood it in my handwriting."

"Yiddish?" Ernest continued.

"It would have been awkward. Did I want a Lubavitcher to intercept it?"

Ernest laughed. "They don't behave that way. To open someone else's letter is a sin."

"Why not in Hebrew?" Rabbi Krausz wondered. I didn't

know how to respond. She continued, "It's *lashon ha-kodesh*, the sacred tongue."

I felt somewhat ashamed.

We began to talk about how the philological study of Hebrew had greatly developed in Germany. She brought out a copy of the *Prolegomena to a Grammar of the Hebrew Language* by David Samuel Luzzatto, first published in Padua in 1836. Pointing at it, she said: "It's an extraordinary disquisition, still among the most erudite. Luzzatto argues that the Spanish period known as La Convivencia, in which Muslim, Jewish, and Christian thinkers cohabited—though not without tension—was fertile in linguistic explorations. In the tenth century, that cohabitation was conducive to Jewish scholars analyzing various Semitic languages in the Torah. The earliest efforts were made by Saadia Gaon, a prominent ninth-century exegete who lived in Palestine and wrote on philosophy, linguistics, and halakha, or Jewish law. [His work *Emunot ve-Deot (Beliefs and Opinions)* sought to reconcile Jewish theology and Greek philosophy and was read with admiration by thinkers like Maimonides.] Saadia Gaon used to say that if Hebrew is not protected, it will perish. 'I have observed that many Jews are not familiar with the purity of our language in its traditional form, all the more so with its difficult words. When they speak many words are incorrect; and when they write poems the ancient elements in them are rare, while those disregarded are numerous.' Such sentiment resonated in the work of Solomon ibn Gabirol, a magnificent poet known to the gentile world as Avicebron. For a long time people didn't know that the author of the philosophical treatise *Fons Vitae* [*Fountain of Life*] was a Jew. Ibn Gabirol believed Hebrew had been destroyed through malpractice. Another scholar was Menachem ben Sarug, who in his dictionary *Mahberet* discussed the language of the Bible––in Hebrew. Similar studies were made by Moses ibn Ezra and Rashi."

Rabbi Krausz described Luzzatto as a member of the Wissenschaft des Judentums, or "Science of Judaism," movement led by Leopold Zunz in nineteenth-century Germany. Zunz was an ordained Reform rabbi who, having found the rabbinate incompatible with secular life, in 1819 created, along with a cadre of intellectuals, a center for the scientific study of Judaism known in German as Verein für Kultur und Wissenschaft der Juden. Together with Heinrich Graetz, Zunz sought to legitimize the study of Judaism as a research discipline. The scholars saw Judaism as a major force in Western civilization. Their focus wasn't only on history, culture, and society. The Hebrew language—its grammar, syntax, and styles—became a source of fascination.

It was Luzzatto who focused on Hebrew. Born in Trieste, he studied Talmud as a child. But he was interested in languages. An extraordinary polyglot, he was the first scholar to study Syriac. An anti-Aristotelian (who disliked Maimonides), he became a passionate student of the Bible. It was he who argued that the book of Ecclesiastes wasn't written by King Solomon but by an author called Kohelet. Rabbi Krausz asserted that Luzzatto and the cadre of Wissenschaft des Judentums pushed Hebrew grammar out of Talmudic discussion and into academia. Their efforts coincided with the early steps in archaeology, made in an effort to understand the past through the examination of surviving artifacts. Not long after Zunz established his center, in 1829, Eduard Gerhard discovered the archaeological foundations of Rome. Other similar excavations and discoveries followed, including a handful connected with Phoenician, Egyptian, and Hebrew inscriptions dating back to prebiblical times.

"Today the study of Hebrew is a science," said Rabbi Krausz. "That's a fairly recent phenomenon."

"But it was aborted in Germany by the Nazis," I added. "Isn't living as a Jew in Berlin like roaming in a cemetery? The city is astonishingly lively, yet the realization that your own ancestors were decimated here must make it bizarre."

"And where haven't they been killed?" wondered Rabbi Krausz.

"Well, that's a tautology!" I exclaimed. "Are you suggesting that Jewish life in the Diaspora ought to be accepted as a sequence of martyrdoms?"

Toward the end of the evening (and a couple of bottles of wine later), the conversation returned to the Golem. In my mind, this mythical creature, not so different from the *Liwerant* of my dream, is closely associated with Jewish life in the Diaspora, since its function is to protect the Jewish community in Prague from its enemies. Gershom Scholem had devoted a chapter in *Major Trends in Jewish Mysticism* to the Golem. Rabbi Krausz reminded me of the meaning of the word in Hebrew: "It appears in Psalms 139:16 to refer to an 'unformed substance.' Or maybe the reference is to an embryo. The word also shows up in the Babylonian Talmud (*Sanhedrin* 38b) to describe the stage in which Adam was before he received the breath of life." She paused. "But in the Mishnah, the term is used to describe an uneducated person, although the reference might be more aggressive: stupid, idiot."

I asked her and Ernest if they knew Borges's poem about the Golem. Here, the middle stanzas in Alan S. Trueblood's translation:

One memory stands out, unlike the rest—
dim shapes always fading from time's dim log.
Still fresh and green the memory persists
of Judah León, a rabbi once in Prague.

Thirsty to know things only known to God,
Judah León shuffled letters endlessly,
trying them out in subtle combinations
till at last he uttered the Name that is the Key,

the Garden, the Echo, the Landlord, and the Mansion,
over a dummy which, with fingers wanting grace,
he fashioned, thinking to teach it the arcane
of Words and Letters and of Time and Space.

The simulacrum lifted its drowsy lids
and, much bewildered, took in color and shape
in a floating world of sounds. Following this,
it hesitantly took a timid step.

I told them I liked the inventiveness of the poem. Given that the *-em* termination is impossible to rhyme in Spanish, Borges shrewdly links the word *Golem* with *Scholem* thus:

> That cabbalist who played at being God
> gave his spacey offspring the nickname Golem.
> (In a learned passage of his volume,
> these truths have been conveyed to us by Scholem.)

I said that the word *Golem* makes people think of androids. For instance, the Golem Project at Brandeis University, in Waltham, Massachusetts, is devoted to the automatic design and manufacture of robotic life-forms. But Rabbi Krausz suggested that the Golem, when approached as a symbol in the context of Jewish culture, needed to be seen as strictly Diasporic. "The Maharal created his creature out of sand because the Jews of Prague needed protection. It's a body-guard, a defender. In Israel, Jews defend themselves. But outside of Israel we're vulnerable."

Her words made me think of the dichotomy between Israel and the Diaspora. After visiting Israel repeatedly, I admired the Israeli tenacity, the gusto people displayed in everything they did. But the country's hypermilitarization, while an expected response to the ongoing threats from its surroundings, saddened me. I had just returned from a week-long trip there, and, again, I was overwhelmed by the amount of security I saw everywhere. One needed to go through a checkpoint to buy a Band-Aid at a pharmacy, drink an espresso, or deposit a check. The green-uniformed soldiers were all-pervasive. The display of strength is essential for a nation under threat.

I thought of a passage from Borges in "The Argentine Writer and Tradition," an essay in which he asks what the Argentine literary tradition ought to be. His answer is swift and categorical: "I believe our tradition is all of Western culture," he says. Borges reiterates his admiration for the Jews and states (paraphrasing sociologist Thorstein Veblen) that the preeminence of Jews in Western civilization comes from the fact that "they act within that culture and, at the same time, do not feel tied to it by any special devotion." Israel, it seems to me, requires a special devotion. Israelis have no need for the Golem because they themselves are warriors.

I told Ernest and Rabbi Krausz that I liked not feeling tied.

"You like being a *luftmensch*!" responded Ernest. "But it's a treacherous position. In the United States, where you live, Jews aren't really outsiders. Yet you can still indulge in your feeling of being free of ties and not having to pay the traditional price for it. You might need a Golem one day. And then what? You don't have the magic to create one. You're vulnerable! You aren't invincible!"

ר

Back in Jerusalem, I made a point of visiting the Church of the Nativity. Hillel Halkin had talked to me about Aramaic during the Roman occupation. And with David Grossman I had discussed the unwavering support that fundamentalist

Christians give Israel. But I had never been to Jesus's birthplace in Bethlehem, in the West Bank. So I made the necessary travel arrangements.

Accompanying me was Eva Hoffman, a Polish-Canadian writer and psychoanalyst originally from Kraków. A few weeks earlier, while in London, I had mentioned my intention to Hoffman when I met her at a literary gathering. Hoffman's parents were Holocaust survivors who hid from the Nazis in the Ukraine. The family emigrated in 1959. Hoffman did her undergraduate studies at Houston's Rice University, went to Yale for a short period of time to study music, and then switched to Harvard, where she obtained a doctorate in literature.

Hoffman and I agreed to meet in the outskirts of Jerusalem at an Arab falafel joint called The House of Pita. There we would wait for our tourist guide to arrive.

The guide was almost an hour late. While we waited and drank herbal tea, I told Hoffman I had enjoyed reading her book about her translingual journey. "You managed to transform exile into an advantage, not a handicap. That transformation," I said, "is a Jewish act."

She responded that nostalgia is the engine that propels much of literature.

I mentioned Psalms 137:5: "If I forget thee, O Jerusalem, let my right hand forget her cunning." To remember is a mandate.

When I said this to Hoffman, she responded, "In some way, it is indeed. The psalm emphasizes memory. Not to remember is to lose the capacity to write."

I told her about my research into Hebrew. "There was a gap of almost two millennia between the destruction of the Second Temple and the creation of the State of Israel. The fact that the language went through such an extended dormant stage is seen by the Zionists as an interruption. But the Rabbis understood better." °

"What do you mean?" she asked.

"How do sperm banks work? Through refrigeration. That is the way the Rabbis protected the sacred tongue, too. They used Hebrew only for theological debate. By doing so, they turned it into myth."

I said that the savviest, most radical transformation of the Exilic period is the production of the Talmud in its parallel editions: the Palestinian (misnamed *Yerushalmi*, although it wasn't redacted in Jerusalem) and the Babylonian. The Talmud became a manual of behavior. "Remember, this is the time when an influential pedagogical system of schooling that became known in Hebrew as *yeshivah* [meaning 'to sit'] was implemented, starting in the early parts of the first millennium C.E. The first academies were in Babylon: Sura and Pumbedita."

Hoffman spoke about these rabbis as immigrants. What was their experience as they traveled to distant lands? "Every immigrant becomes an amateur anthropologist," she said. "Arriving late to a culture allows for a certain distance from it, a sense of perspective."

The Rabbis' dilemma, I replied, needed to be seen against the backdrop of a majority-minority divide. "Take Rashi, who lived in eleventh-century France. To what extent was

Rashi defined by the culture that surrounded him? To a very limited one, I think. His environment was mostly limited to things Jewish."

"But he was an exile," Hoffman said. "Not being French doesn't mean he wasn't in France."

We talked about the two of us writing in a neutral language—English—that isn't our mother tongue.

"Jews have been doing it for centuries," she said.

I mentioned the dream I had had about Hebrew and that I had been exploring the place of Eliezer Ben-Yehuda in the Israeli imagination. "At one point in his autobiography," I said to Hoffman, "Ben-Yehuda talks about switching tongues. From Yiddish and Russian, he turned to Hebrew. In other words, to revive a language he needed to sacrifice another—maybe more than one. But he's peculiar in his attitude. Having been a polyglot, he wants to become monolingual. The implication of this switch irks me. It's a reversal of the legend of the Tower of Babel. Hebrew, and only Hebrew, is what he wants. He says that Hebrew became his language not only at the verbal level but in thought. 'I think in Hebrew by day and by night, awake and in dreams, in sickness and in health, and even when I am racked with pain.' "

"Maybe it's true."

"You doubt it?" I asked.

"He sounds like a monomaniac."

"Stanisław Barańczak, the Polish translator of the Nobel Prize–winner Wisława Szymborska, once said that a writer who switches languages never masters any of them," I said.

"I agree," commented Hoffman. "At least it seems impossible to internalize a second language as fully as the first."

"The truth is, no language can ever be mastered," I said. "Look at Nabokov. His English is stilted. And I'm told by a Russian scholar who specializes in his novels that the same is true in Russian. Samuel Beckett's French was foreign, too."

"Yes, but all of them wrote as translators."

"What do you mean?"

"To switch languages is to become conscious of the mechanics behind the words. That's what translators need to know in order to do their job. Writers who switch languages are, in some way, their own translators."

"Yes," I said. "And I think that all Diasporic Jews, be they writers or not, have that experience, too. Even if they are monolingual, they have a relationship with language that's schizophrenic. It's in a constant state of unfolding.

"Translation is a Jewish way of life," I added. I told Hoffman about a letter that Samuel ibn Tibbon had written to Maimonides asking him for permission to translate his book *The Guide for the Perplexed*, which was drafted in the philosophical language of the time: Arabic. The book was already in Hebrew but in a poor version. Trying to impress Maimonides, Ibn Tibbon summarized his accomplishments. Maimonides praised his correspondent: "You're thoroughly fitted for the task of translation," he said, "because the Creator has given you an intelligent mind to understand parables and their interpretation, the words of the wise and their difficult sayings."

"In other words, to be a translator requires the person to be specially attuned to things," I suggested to Hoffman. "In fact, Maimonides emphasizes clarity as a sine qua non for the task. It's easy to translate word by word, but no clarity will result from such mechanics. He said that the translator should first try to grasp the sense of the passage thoroughly, and then state the author's intention with perfect clarity. This, however, cannot be done without changing the order of words, putting many words for one, or vice versa, and adding or taking away words, so that the subject may be as clear and perfectly intelligible in the language into which he translates."

Finally our tourist guide—his name was Naim L.— showed up, apologizing profusely for the delay. He drove us in his blue Mazda to a checkpoint, where Hoffman and I showed our passports and Naim displayed an ID.

Naim was a handsome man in his thirties. He wore his hair short. His most distinctive features were his thick glasses and his yarmulke, which had the word *Israel* embroidered in graffiti letters. He was a student doing advanced work in archaeology at the Hebrew University. He first took us to Rachel's tomb in the outskirts of Bethlehem and then to the Church of the Nativity. As we walked around the church, which covers approximately 129,000 square feet, he pointed out the historical significance of its various aspects, detailing how the mother of Emperor Constantine, Saint Helena, had begun the first basilica. The edifice was completed in the year 333, but it burned down two centuries later during the Samaritan Revolt. He explained that the current building dated back to 565. It had been built by Justinian I.

I asked Naim if, as Halkin told me earlier, Jesus had spoken a bastardized Aramaic with a strong Greek influence. He said that during the Roman control of Palestine, at the time of Jesus, Aramaic was indeed the common language, although Hebrew and Greek were in use, too. Jewish life under occupation was challenging. It was also multifaceted. Just as in contemporary Israel there are varieties of Hebrew spoken in different quarters, at the time of Jesus people used various Aramaic dialects: Galilean Aramaic in Galilee, Samaritan Aramaic in Samaria, and Rabbinic Hebrew in Judea, the latter a variety already pushing away from biblical Hebrew.

Hoffman raised the topic of the Dead Sea Scrolls. The museum housing them, called the Shrine of the Book, is in Jerusalem, and she intended to visit it soon. Naim explained that the scrolls had been discovered in a group of Qumran caves between 1947 and 1956, and are an invaluable source for understanding Hebrew at the time. The various pieces covered approximately three hundred years, from about 250 B.C.E. to 68 C.E. "Their content offers a glimpse of extreme theological views at the time of Roman rule," Naim said, "including those manifested in the Apocrypha and Pseudepigrapha. In fact, through them it's possible to appreciate the way the language was written, the various dialects in circulation at the time, and the influence of Aramaic on Hebrew, particularly the Samarian type."

There were plenty of Christian tourists near us as we made our way to the church nave. From there we proceeded to visit the silver star beneath the altar in the grotto of the church. The star marks the exact location where Jesus was born.

Pointing in its direction, Naim said, "There it is, the

navel of the world! I don't think I'll go down. I've seen it a zillion times. I'll wait outside."

Going down needed to be done in orderly fashion, one person at a time. There were stairs to be taken, an experience that made me think of Borges descending into the basement to see the *aleph*.

There was a line of people. Hoffman told me to go first. She waited for her turn outside.

What I saw when I took the stairs and reached the bottom floor looked like a small-scale Grand Guignol theater. It was defined by a purple curtain with white designs and yellow fringes. The stage, shaped as a semicircle, was made of marble broken into segments. The marble was speckled brown. Inside the theater were silver cups, a pair of flat candleholders, and the silver star. The place was airless. It exuded a stale smell that reminded me of burnt rubber.

I reemerged and saw Hoffman awaiting her turn to go down. "Hard to believe a little hole in the ground is the source of such adoration," I commented.

"And what about the Wailing Wall?" she replied.

I immediately thought of Grossman's comment to me about the power of stones in Israel, though it was harnessing that power to words that had been the key to Ben-Yehuda's achievement.

After the visit, the three of us went back to Jerusalem in Naim's Mazda. Once we had dropped Hoffman off at the bus station, Naim and I continued our conversation as we made our way to my hotel. I told him the reason for my visit to Israel and mentioned Ben-Yehuda.

"You're looking for the wrong person," Naim insisted. "How about Bialik? He had far more intellectual power. Did you ever read his poem 'City of the Killings' ['*Be'Ir ha-Haregah*']? It was written in 1904 to eulogize a massacre known as the Kishinev pogrom. Kishinev was the capital of the Bessarabian province. The pogrom was a watershed for Zionists. It was triggered by a Christian boy being murdered. Although the killer was one of the boy's relatives, the anti-Semitic media propagated the idea that the Jews had committed the crime. Close to fifty Jews were massacred and almost a hundred were gravely wounded. Bialik was sent to Kishinev by the Jewish Historical Commission to interview survivors. His impressions were stamped in the poem. His diction was astoundingly flexible. And more than Ben-Yehuda, Bialik was a master at coining beautiful neologisms while building a bridge with the biblical past. How about his 'On the Slaughter' ['*Al ha-Sh'chitah*'], written in the tradition of a biblical lament? It is a more succinct poem, rebelling against a God who, in Bialik's view, stands still as Jews are murdered. There's an overt disillusionment with religion. Spiritually dry, the poet wonders what value faith has in a world ruled by violence."

Later, I consulted the original in the National Library. The cadence in Hebrew is incantatory. Here are the first and last stanzas, in T. Carmi's English translation:

> Heaven, beg mercy for me! If there is
> a God in you, and a pathway through
> you in this God—which I have not

discovered—then pray for me! For my
heart is dead, no longer is that prayer
on my lips; all strength is gone, how
much longer, until when?

. . . .

And cursed be the man who says:
Avenge! No such revenge—revenge for
the blood of a little child—has yet been
devised by Satan. Let the blood pierce
through the abyss! Let the blood seep
down to the depths of darkness, and
eat away there, in the dark, and breach
all the rotting foundations of the earth.

"It's far more interesting than anything Ben-Yehuda ever
did," said Naim. "That's because Ben-Yehuda was a phony,"
he added.

"Why?"

"He didn't have any talents. What talent do you need to
browse through books and make lists? That's what he's
remembered for: making lists. He used the Bible for his own
purposes but didn't really understand it. Bialik, instead, was
appreciative of it. You know what Bialik said about the
Torah? That it made a nation of the Jewish people. Now
that's a revolutionary thought! For him the dictum that
'Israel and the Torah are one' was no mere phrase. He said
that the content and connotations of the Torah embrace
more than 'religion' or 'creed' alone, or 'ethics' or 'commandments' or 'learning' alone, and it is not even just a

combination of all these, but something far transcending all of them. He said it's a mystical, almost cosmic, conception. 'The Torah is the tool of the Creator; with it and for it He created the universe. It is the highest idea. Without it the world would not exist and would have no right to exist.' "

It seemed to me that Naim was turning Bialik into a religious fanatic.

"Not at all," he replied. "Bialik himself said that knowledge of the Torah ranks higher than priesthood or kingship. He believed that only he is free who engages in the study of the Torah. It might sound extreme, but Bialik made poetry out of this view. Ben-Yehuda did nothing remotely close."

"I'm taken by the passion Israelis have for poetry," I said, mentioning the waitress with the Iranian accent who had recited to me Yehuda Amichai's poem about the diameter of a bomb.

"Yes, poetry matters here. But the mystical side of the language has become a casualty. How many people have you come across in Israel that can talk to you about the *Sephirot*, a word that means 'sphere' as well as 'numerations,' but that, understood properly, offers a model of mystical transcendence? How many know of the *Adam Kadmon*, the hierarchical organization of the universe that is the base of Kabbalah and announces that the human body has power entities called *Sephirot* (*Keter*, *Binah*, *Hokhmah*, *Da'at*, *Gevurah*, on and on until one reaches *Malkhut*) with counterparts in the natural world. Like other nations, Israelis are practical people. They don't want to waste time on ethereal things. Read Ben-Yehuda's work carefully. You won't find more than a passing reference to mysticism. He thoroughly disliked it. For him letters were letters were letters.

"Bialik, on the other hand," Naim continued, "always called attention to the spiritual aspect of the Hebrew language. Like Ben-Yehuda, he hated passivity; yet he was savvy enough to understand that there are higher levels of consciousness. His hatred of passivity, he suggested, involved a rediscovery of the Hebrew alphabet that Jews needed to engage in. Together with his friend the editor Yehoshua Hana Ravnitzky, Bialik produced an ambitious anthology called *Sefer ha-Aggadah* [*Book of Legend*], a three-volume effort published between 1908 and 1911, in which he revised classic Jewish legends, adapting them for the modern reader. His objective was to reconnect his audience, the Jews in the Pale of Settlement and those in Palestine, with esoteric wisdom, establishing a connection for modernism with its Rabbinic roots. There is a telling passage in Bialik's anthology, adapted from the Talmud (*Shabbat* 119b), that plays upon the sound of the name of each letter and a word starting with, and connected to, it."

Later on, I found the passage Naim was referring to in William G. Braude's English version:

The sages said to Rabbi Joshua ben Levi [scholar of the first half of the third century c.e.]: Today some young children came to the house of study and told us things the like of which had not been said even in the days of Joshua son of Nun:

Alef means "Learn wisdom (*alef binah*)."

Gimel and *dalet* mean "Be kind to the poor (*gemol dal-*

lim)." Why is the foot of the *gimel* stretched toward the base of the *dalet*? Because it is the way of the benevolent to run after the poor [to help them out].

And why is the foot of the *dalet* stretched toward the *gimel*? Because the poor must make himself available to the benevolent.

And why is the face of the *dalet* averted from the *gimel*? Because help must be given in secrecy, so that the poor will not be humiliated by the presence of the giver.

And,

> *Shin* stands for "falsehood" (*sheker*), and *tav* for "truth" (*emet*). Why do the letters of *sheker* in the alphabet closely follow one another, while the letters of *emet* are far apart? Because falsehoods follow close upon one another, while truth is encountered only at intervals far apart.
>
> And why does *sheker* (falsehood) stand on one leg, while *emet* (truth) is made up of the letters *alef, mem,* and *tav*, which have [solid] bricklike bases? Because truth stands firmly; falsehood does not.

Truth stands firmly; falsehood does not. Bialik was truthful. Hebraists like Eliezer Ben-Yehuda might have perceived themselves as messianic in political terms, but the psychological map of the Jews is more intricate. You cannot ignore the spirit while emphasizing the mundane. Your soul will break in half!

Before Naim dropped me off, he told me, "Without Ben-

Yehuda, Hebrew would still be what it is today: the official language of the Jewish State. But without Bialik, we would be far poorer."

ש

That night, my head filled with Jesus, Ben-Yehuda, and Bialik, I found it hard to sleep. I turned on the TV and spent a few minutes flipping from one channel to another. The programming was in multiple languages. There was a talk show in German about prostitution; a political panel in Hebrew on the forthcoming fortieth anniversary of the Six-Day War, to take place a week later; a *telenovela* from Venezuela (or maybe from Mexico); the news in Arabic, detailing a series of suicide bombings in Baghdad markets, along with interviews with a Shiite cleric about the destruction of a mosque; and a documentary in Russian on Vladimir Putin. I also caught a summary of the day's international sports events, including a long argument between two Israeli commentators about a recent goal by the center forward from the soccer team Maccabi Tel Aviv. The goal appeared to have been scored unlawfully. It was clear from the replays that the player had used a combination of his head and his right hand to push the ball into the net. In the discussion, one of the commentators brought up an episode in a notorious match between Argentina and England that took place in the 1986 World Cup. In the final score, Argentina won 2–1. The first Argentine goal was scored by Diego Armando Maradona, with his hand, but the referee didn't see the infraction.

Later, during an interview, Maradona said that the goal was scored "a little with the head of Maradona and a little with the hand of God." The Israeli commentator repeated that sentence at least three times, modifying it each time: "A little with one's head and a little with God's hand."

I took a hot bath and opened one of the Ben-Yehuda biographies I had brought with me. In a nearby room, a party was going on. For a second I thought of dialing the hotel's reception desk to complain. But I let it pass. I closed my book and turned the light off again. An ambulance was passing by on the street. I tried sleeping again.

That's when I had my second dream. The longer I reflect on it, the more I'm convinced it's a response to the one that had come to me years before, prompting me to reevaluate my relationship with Hebrew.

In the dream I was in a small, metallic elevator that kept on going up and down without reason, in spite of my effort to control its movements. I was supposed to exit the elevator on the thirteenth floor, but only twelve numbers were listed. "Maybe the architect had already designed the building and the elevator was put in as an afterthought," I mused.

Every time I pushed a button, its doors opened. But in front of me there were bricks. Obviously, the doors weren't properly synchronized. Trying to coordinate them with an exit, I kept pushing different buttons—to no avail. I gave up in frustration, kneeling on the floor while trying to think of an alternative. The doors were closed.

I turned around and looked down at my shoes. They were an old pair, but their soles appeared intact. "I'm in luck!" I said to myself.

Suddenly I heard someone screaming from outside the elevator. It was a guttural masculine voice. I imagined its owner as an obese opera singer. "It's an emergency. You must get out because your father is gravely ill. His lungs no longer function. He's out of breath. Your father is waiting for you."

I was shaken. "Where is he?" I asked.

No answer.

"Will he survive?"

"His soul is being tested. Maybe God's hand will help him," replied the voice.

"I'm happy," I answered. "My father speaks a flawless Hebrew." Yet just as I uttered the sentence, I realized I had lied. My father doesn't speak a word of Hebrew—not a word. The best he might be able to do is gather a handful of expressions from his Yiddish. He was in Israel during his honeymoon, almost fifty years ago. It was 1960. The country was still young, and so was he.

"I should be able to translate for him," I thought.

But could I? He might be dead by the time I reach him . . .

ת

When I next saw Nowodworski, he asked me if I had become saturated with Ben-Yehuda. "Does he still matter to you?"

"I need to see his tomb," I responded.

Two days later, I made my way to the Mount of Olives.

In my travels I regularly allow a couple of hours to wander around the local Jewish cemetery. I might have a relative in it. But even when I don't, I feel the need to have an encounter with the dead, to be in dialogue with them. I walk around reading the stone inscriptions, trying to decipher through the meager information they display (name, dates of birth and death, a logo such as a hand, a menorah, a lion, and the Ten Commandments, maybe a photograph, and an epitaph that defined them) their entire weltanschauung. Did they die young? Might their deaths have been an accident? Is the tomb situated near the tomb of a beloved one? If so, do they share a death date?

In Prague I visited the Old Cemetery in Josefov, the Jewish Quarter. It contains approximately twelve thousand graves and was used between 1478 and 1787. This is where the maker of the Golem, Rabbi Judah Loew, rests for eternity. The site is hypnotizing. In a small piece of real estate, tombstones, covered with mold, pile on top of one another. The visitor needs to walk through overgrown weeds to read the inscriptions. The Hebrew letters engraved on the stones are disappearing. How much longer will they last? Prague is where the Nazis placed the treasures they looted from Jewish homes across Europe. The city was to be a living museum, but it's in the Old Cemetery where souls seem to dance, decrying the abuses of history.

The opposite is true of Warsaw's Jewish cemetery, on Okopowa Street. It's one of the largest in Europe: eighty-three acres long. Established in 1806, it has been the target of repeated desecrations. Its tombs are disfigured, broken into pieces. No vandals have ever been caught. My relatives on the Altchuler side (my father's maternal line) rest in it. Although I've strolled around—so have my parents, an uncle, and three cousins—the exact locations of their tombs remain unknown.

Years ago, I sought the grave of Edmund Wilson, the pre-eminent literary critic for *The New Yorker* about whom I had spoken to David Grossman. I had read somewhere that Wilson's tombstone displayed a line in Hebrew, and I wanted to see it for myself. In the cemetery in Wellfleet, Massachusetts, where Wilson is buried, the oldest graves date back to the eighteenth century and belong mostly to fishermen. In contrast, Wilson's grave is relatively new—but the inscription is old: "*Hazak, hazak venithazek*" in Hebrew ("Be strong, be strong, and be strengthened").

Maybe I'm fascinated with Jewish graveyards because of their centrifugal quality. How to explain it? It feels as if energy is sucked into them. I never find them creepy. Nor do I get scared. They symbolize roots. To bury a relative is to make the soil sacred. Israel is already sacred. Cemeteries like the one on the Mount of Olives are an extension of that sacredness. But in the Diaspora Jewish sacredness is an anomaly. It's found only in synagogues and cemeteries. Jews are allowed to pray anywhere, and that act makes the place holy. But a synagogue isn't an *anywhere*; it's a locus of faith.

Not that sacredness and fallibility aren't compatible. Over time, I've come across mistakes on gravestones: a name spelled differently on the front and back of the stone, with a *lamed* instead of a *nun*; the wrong Jewish date quoted against the Gregorian calendar; a Star of David poorly executed.

Some of those errors might be appropriate. The Beth El Cemetery, in Paramus, New Jersey, isn't particularly appealing. Still, I visited it because, among other reasons, Isaac Bashevis Singer is buried there. There's a humorous anecdote about Singer's tombstone inscription. The epitaph originally stated in English: "*Noble* Laureate." Noble? Having done extensive work on him, it wouldn't be my first choice of adjectives to describe him. He was abrasive, presumptuous, and egomaniacal. In any case, the carver had meant *Nobel*. It took half a dozen years for the typo to be corrected.

My roots—where are they?

In Israel *and* in Mexico. On the Mount of Olives and in the Ashkenazic cemetery on Calle Constituyentes.

And how will my epitaph read?

It should be a line from the Talmud (*Berakhot* 57b), written in Hebrew characters:

Sleep is a sixtieth of death.

Before Eliezer Ben-Yehuda came along, Hebrew had been asleep for centuries. Maybe not fully asleep. His was the generation that brought it back, resurrecting it from the dead. The concept of resurrection might seem like an oxymoron in Judaism, but the idea is deeply Jewish. Jews recite the phrase "Blessed are you God who revives the dead" as part of the daily liturgy. Ezekiel is shown a vision of the scattered Jews, in exile after the destruction of the First Temple, as dry bones that begin to rise and live before the prophet's eyes. And in Daniel 12:1–2, it is stated that the time will come when the People of Israel "that sleep in the dust of the earth shall awake, some to everlasting life, and some to shame and everlasting contempt." According to the Bible, deliverance will take place at the Mount of Olives, the site where Jews will collectively wake up.

The Mount of Olives is in East Jerusalem. The cemetery is at its top. It has a sacrosanct air to it. Its white-stone style makes the visitor feel cleansed. This is the place where the Roman soldiers camped during the siege of the city, which they ended up destroying in the first century C.E. And just below is the Garden of Gethsemane, where, according to the New Testament, Jesus and his disciples retreated to pray during the Last Supper; thus, it is regularly visited by Christian pilgrims. Mary's tomb is said to be in the mountain, as is the tomb of Zechariah Ben-Jehoiada, who, as stated in II Chronicles 24:20–21, was stoned to death on the order of King Jehoash. Other notable people buried in the Mount of Olives include politicians such as Menachem Begin, theologians such as Aryeh Kaplan and Abraham Isaac Kook, and writers such as Agnon and Uri Zvi Greenberg.

Ben-Yehuda's funeral occurred on a rainy winter day. The procession was made up of some thirty thousand people from a variety of backgrounds: men and women; Yemenites, Sephardim, and Ashkenazim; Zionists and the Orthodox; Arab workers, Turk administrators, and the British elite. The mood was somber. A huge crowd of hats, umbrellas, and flags—no individual faces are identified in the photo I saw of the event—moved down a narrow street.

St. John, who interviewed Ben-Yehuda's close circle, says that the family wasn't allowed to follow the cortege. Although he didn't leave a will, Ben-Yehuda had spoken about wanting to be cremated, which is forbidden by Jewish law. The reason he changed his mind, I suspect, is that he probably wanted to avert any confrontation his wife and children might later have with the religious establishment. (Recall that when his first wife, Dvora, died, the Orthodox refused to have her buried in a Jewish cemetery, arguing that the family wasn't Jewish enough.) In any case, a funeral for such a national figure could only be strictly kosher. St. John says that it was Ben-Yehuda's widow who chose the spot for the burial on the Mount of Olives. "It was a favorite of both," St. John writes, "where they often sat together to rest."

As I stood next to Ben-Yehuda's grave, I tried to visualize the young nation as it stopped to mourn the man who had persuaded everyone that Hebrew was the way to the future. I had seen images of Ben-Yehuda in the work of Ya'akov Ben-Dov, known as the father of Hebrew film. Ben-Dov immigrated in 1907, as part of the Second Aliyah, and with a camera documented the building of the Jewish State in the early days of the twentieth century. I'd seen his vivid footage of the period—originally released in the films *Shivat Tzion* (*Return to Zion*, 1920), *Eretz Yisrael ha-Mitchadeshet* (*Rebirth of a New Palestine*, 1923), and *Aviv b'Eretz Yisrael* (*Romance in Palestine*, 1928), and assembled into a single film by Ya'akov Gross in 1997, titled *Bonim v'Lohamim* (*Builders and Fighters*). Pioneers planting trees and building wooden structures, orphans at school, immigrants arriving by boat in Jaffa, camels, soldiers, a marching band, an archaeological expedition excavating biblical ruins, a pair of men boxing . . . The film is a *rezenptiongeschichte* of Ben-Yehuda and the way his iconic personality captivated the people of his age.

In Ben-Dov's footage, Ben-Yehuda is seen breaking ground for a new house he's ready to build in the Talpiot neighborhood in Jerusalem, with money given to him by American Jews during his trip to work at the New York Public Library. He is also featured next to Winston Churchill, Lawrence of Arabia, and Sir Herbert Samuel, the British high commissioner in Palestine. Samuel was a Jew, a fact that delighted Ben-Yehuda, because to him it symbolized the passing of the political torch from gentile to Jewish hands. He called Samuel "the King of Israel," even though, at the end of his life, Ben-Yehuda was critical of the high commissioner for his inefficacy in brokering a Jewish-Arab coalition.

Ben-Yehuda's tomb is sparse. It lies horizontally and is surrounded by a low fence. It looks down on the Temple area and the Golden Gate. The inscription is in old Hebrew. And it's inscribed with a map of Israel in the shape of a house.

Standing in front of it, alone, I said to myself: "So here's where God's helper was finally put to rest. He was a traveler, too: from Luzhky to Plotzk, from Dünaburg to Paris, from Turkey to Haifa, from London to Moscow, from Cairo to Helsinki, from Manhattan to Algiers, he traversed the routes that were important in his day and age. In that transit, he made Jerusalem his epicenter. And in the end he found rest in the Mount of Olives. From this place Ben-Yehuda forever contemplates the fruits of his labor. His dream has come true. But can he still claim it as his own?"

My odyssey had started in a dream about language withdrawal, as my friend had called it. Trying to explain it to myself had become a journey of discovery—with Ben-Yehuda at the wheel. I now understood that losing my Hebrew wasn't only about forgetting and remembering words. It was about the nature of language as a whole—and about Hebrew as an indisputable conduit, the radar of Jewish identity. In the last several years, I had made an effort to recover the Hebrew of my schooling in Mexico, the Hebrew I had used when I lived in Israel for a year in the late seventies, the Hebrew of my ancestors and descendants, the Hebrew that connected me and every Jew who has ever lived with the generation at Mount Sinai.

During my search, I had spoken Hebrew with teachers, waiters, taxi drivers, lexicographers, rabbis, and kibbutzniks. But I had also used other tongues, as many as I was able to grasp. That plethora, and the restlessness that pushed me to meet another conversant somewhere in the globe, made me a Diasporic Jew. I realized that my search for Hebrew was for something far more multifarious than a language. The Hebrew of my dream wasn't only a system of sounds; it was an existential condition, a way of being, of establishing contact with others, with God, and with myself.

In Beit Hatefusoth, the museum dedicated to the Jewish Diaspora located at Tel Aviv University, I had seen a documentary about the twenty-five-hundred-year Jewish journey from Canaan to . . . where? The filmmakers, in their Zionist zeal, presented the multiple Jewish communities in the world as self-sufficient yet incomplete in their existence until they made aliyah. Ascendance to Israel was the only road to salvation. But the Israel I had rediscovered for myself in my successive visits was a fractured place, divided into endless subcategories, in a constant state of change. In it one never got the sense of coming to the end of history. On the contrary, the country is a work in progress.

Some parts of my dream had become intelligible. But dreams aren't rational thoughts that appear to us in a different wrapping. They have their own logic. Some parts of them make sense; others never do. Not everything in life has to be coherent.

Earlier I had told Eliezer Nowodworski, my invaluable guide, that after so much walking and talking in Israel and elsewhere, I appreciated better the message that my dream had attempted to deliver to me. The two of us were on a train headed to Jerusalem. A young soldier was sitting to my right, his rifle inadvertently digging into my left knee.

"Do you remember the song by Chava Alberstein that I sang to you?" asked Nowodworski.

"Yes."

"Running the risk of sounding like a music box, I have another one for you." He handed me a CD. "I bought it this morning. It's called '*Holem be-Sfardait*,' 'I Dream in Spanish.' It was written by Ehud Manor for Shlomo Yidov, a fellow *porteño* who attended Sholem Aleikhem Shul in Buenos Aires until his aliyah, the same school I attended some years later. Listen to it on your iPod when you get a chance. Yidov says in it that although he thinks and speaks effortlessly in Hebrew and has every word he needs at his disposal, he still dreams in Spanish: *en español*. It's the reverse of you!"

Legend has it that Eliezer Ben-Yehuda died while working in his *Milon* on the word *nefesh*, the Hebrew word for "soul." Undoubtedly, it's a crucial word, especially since in its modern conception it distinguishes humans from other creatures. But in the Torah it is used to describe living beings. (For instance, "And God created great whales, and every living creature [*nefesh*] that moveth, which the waters brought forth abundantly, after their kind, and every winged fowl after his kind: and God saw that it was good" [Genesis 1:21]. Or, "Whatsoever Adam called every living creature [*nefesh*], that was the name thereof" [Genesis 2:19].)

By the end, Ben-Yehuda had been vilified by different types of Jews, Zionist and non-Zionist, Ashkenazic and Sephardic, religious and secular, in Palestine and abroad. Still, his funeral was attended by approximately thirty thousand people. According to St. John, the casket was followed to the grave by "school children with black-draped flags, ultra-religious Jews with long side curls and garments reminiscent of the ghettos of Europe, Jewish businessmen, very Western-looking, from Tel Aviv and Haifa, healthy young pioneers who had been streaming in for two days from remote colonies, Jewish soldiers, Jewish scholars, Jewish statesmen. There were Christians and Arabs in the procession, and British high officials, Dominican monks and Franciscan monks and Moslem leaders. Palestine was ordered to observe three days of national mourning. Palestine wept."

While looking at Ben-Yehuda's gravestone, I had discovered traces of paint sprayed on it. It had been painted over, graffiti-like. When I later asked an acquaintance about it, she told me that the desecration had taken place several times over, committed not by hoodlums, not by Arabs, but by fanatical religious Jews.

I laughed.

She added that when one of Ben-Yehuda's relatives was given the news, she had inquired: "In what language was the graffiti splashed on?"

"In Hebrew."

"Ah, then Ben-Yehuda won."

ACKNOWLEDGMENTS

I must offer my heartfelt gratitude to Jonathan Rosen for being at my side throughout my journey in search of the meaning of Hebrew. I can't think of a more astute, informed, and devoted editor. Dan Frank at Random House read the manuscript, offering insightful comments. Rahel Lerner also made valuable suggestions. For years Altie Karper at Schocken Books has been my compass. My dear friends Hillel Halkin and Eliezer Nowodworski accompanied me, not only physically but spiritually, during my Israeli sojourn. I appreciate their time and vision.

I also benefited from the company and thoughtful ideas of André Aciman, Orly Albeck, Verónica Albin, Harold Augenbraum, Peter Cole, Justin David, Ariel Dorfman, Joshua Ellison, Nora Gerard, Matthew Glassman, David Grossman, Eva Hoffman, Steven G. Kellman, Stacy Klein, Ernest Klingman, Rebecca Krausz, Naim L., Aaron Lansky, Ivonne Lerner, Alberto Madrona Fernández, Dr. Faruq Mawasi, Alana Newhouse, Amos Oz, Aviezer Ravitzky, Raanan Rein, Esther Rollansky, Ruvik Rosental, David G. Roskies, Doron Rubinstein, Rachel Rubinstein, Angel Sáenz-Badillos, Ken Schoen, Esther H. Schor, Howard Schwartz, Anton Shammas, Rosalie and David Sitman, Neal Sokol, Werner Sollors, Professor Bernard Spolsky, Professor Abraham Tal, Judit

Targarona, Chava Turniansky, Ury Vainsencher, Oscar Villalon, Matthew Warshawsky, Hana Wirth-Nesher, and A. B. Yehoshua. I'm all the better because of them.

My gratitude to Rahel Lerner for the preparation of the chronology.

On Eliezer Ben-Yehuda, I made use of his *Ad Eimatai Dibberu Ivrit?* (1919); *Yisrael le-Arzo ve-li-Leshono* (1929); *Milon ha-lashon ha-Ivrit* (1940); *Avot ha-Lashon ha-Ivrit* (1945); and *A Dream Come True* (1993), translated into English by T. Muraoka, edited by George Mandel. I also was served by the biographical and critical studies *Eliezer Ben-Yehuda: Toledotav u-Mifal Hayyav* (1939), by Joseph Klausner; *Tongue of the Prophets: The Life Story of Eliezer Ben Yehuda* (1952), by Robert St. John; *Rebirth: The Story of Eliezer Ben-Yehudah and the Modern Hebrew Language* (1972), by Dvorah Omer, translated by Ruth Rasnic; and *The Revival of a Classical Tongue: Eliezer Ben Yehuda and the Modern Hebrew Language* (1973), by Jack Fellman.

My knowledge of the history and development of Hebrew, Zionism, and polyglot Jewish life, and the connection between Hebrew and other languages in Israel, owes a debt to a variety of sources, such as *The German Attack on the Hebrew Schools in Palestine* (1918), by Israel Cohen; "A Statistical Analysis of the Revival of Hebrew in Israel," in *Scripta Hierosolymitana* (1956); *Hebrew: The Eternal Language* (1957), by William Chomsky; *The Zionist Idea: A Historical Analysis and Reader* (1959), edited by Arthur Hertzberg; *A Short History of the Hebrew Language* (1973), by Haim Rabin; *Jewish Languages: Themes and Variations* (1978), edited by Herbert H. Paper; *His-*

tory of the Yiddish Language (1980), by Max Weinreich; *A History of the Hebrew Language* (1982), by Eduard Yechezkel Kutscher, edited by Raphael Kutscher; *Readings in the Sociology of Jewish Languages* (1985), edited by Joshua A. Fishman; *The Languages of Jerusalem* (1991), edited by Bernard Spolsky and Robert L. Cooper; *Language in Time of Revolution* (1993), by Benjamin Harshav; *A History of the Hebrew Language* (1993), by Angel Sáenz-Badillos, translated by John Elwolde; "The Situation of Arabic in Israel," by Bernard Spolsky, in *Arabic Sociolinguistics: Issues and Perspectives* (1994), edited by Yasir Suleiman; *Messianism, Zionism, and Jewish Religious Radicalism* (1996), by Aviezer Ravitzky, translated by Michael Swirsky and Jonathan Chipman; *The Languages of Israel: Policy, Ideology, and Practice* (1999), edited by Bernard Spolsky and Elana Shohamy; *Language Contact and Lexical Enrichment in Israeli Hebrew* (2003), by Ghil'ad Zuckermann; and *In the Beginning: A Short History of the Hebrew Language* (2004), by Joel M. Hoffman.

The position paper submitted in 1994 by Elena Shohamy and Bernard Spolsky to the Israeli Ministry of Education was titled "A New Language Policy for Israel."

The exchange between Anton Shammas and A. B. Yehoshua is quoted from *Sleeping on a Wire: Conversations with Palestinians in Israel* (1993), by David Grossman, translated by Haim Watzman.

The anecdote about Haim Blac's daughter attending a performance of George Bernard Shaw's *Pygmalion* is recounted in Ghil'ad Zuckermann's article in the *Australian Journal of Jewish Studies*.

Acknowledgments

The list of Jewish languages given by Professor Spolsky is featured in "From Monolingual to Multilingual? Education Language Policy in Israel," by Elana Shohamy and Bernard Spolsky, in *Corpus Linguistics and Modern Hebrew: Towards the Compilation of the Corpus of Spoken Israeli Hebrew (CoSIH)* (2003), edited by Benjamin H. Hary, as well as in Professor Spolsky's essay "Israel and the Jewish Languages," in *Sociolinguistics: International Handbook of the Science of Language and Society* (2006), edited by Ulrich Ammon, Norbert Dittmar, Klaus J. Mattheier, and Peter Trudgill.

References to Joseph Klausner's lexicographical efforts come from Amos Oz's autobiography *A Tale of Love and Darkness* (2004), translated by Nicholas de Lange.

The web address for the Academy of the Hebrew Language, where the Historical Dictionary Project is described, is http://hebrew-academy.huji.ac.il.

The original names of Rabbi Rebecca Krausz and Naim L. have been changed.

The estimated Jewish population in 1900 quoted in chapter ד is from the Jewish Virtual Library, a division of the American-Israeli Cooperative Enterprise.

The songs "Eliezer Ben-Yehuda" by Yaron London and *"Der alef-beyz"* by Mark Varshavsky were translated into English by Malka Tischler and Max Rosenfeld, respectively.

The midrash in chapter ע is quoted from Howard Schwartz's *Tree of Souls: The Mythology of Judaism* (2004).

I conclude with a quote from George Steiner (*After Babel*, 1975): "Language is the main instrument of man's refusal to accept the world as it is."

CHRONOLOGY

ca. 1700 B.C.E. Written language begins to evolve from pictorial symbols to alphabets.

ca. 1011–971 B.C.E. Reign of King David over a united kingdom with its Hebrew-speaking capital, Jerusalem.

586 B.C.E. Destruction of Jerusalem Temple and beginning of Babylonian exile.

ca. 536 B.C.E. Beginning of return of Jews to the land of Israel and rebuilding of Temple.

ca. 500 B.C.E. Beginning of canonization of the Bible.

70 C.E. Destruction of the Second Temple by the Romans; likely the end of the period of biblical Hebrew.

ca. 100 C.E. Completion of process of canonization of the *Tanakh*.

132–135 C.E. The Bar Kochba revolt against the Romans is one of the last attempts to regain Jewish sovereignty in the land of

Israel; surviving letters from this period
are written in Mishnaic Hebrew, which
had probably existed as a spoken
vernacular for several centuries.

ca. fifth century Hesychius of Alexandria creates the most
important Greek lexicon from antiquity.

ca. 902 At age twenty, Saadia Gaon, an Egyptian-
born Jew who will become leader of
Talmudic academy in Babylonian city of
Sura and first significant Jewish
philosopher of the medieval period,
publishes *Sefer ha-Agron*, the first of
several works on the Hebrew language.
Sefer ha-Agron was expanded several years
later and included a Hebrew dictionary
and a rhyming dictionary to aid poets.

ca. 1135 Moses ibn Ezra, a great medieval poet
born in Granada, publishes *Kitab al-
Muhadara wa al-Mudhakara*, one of the
earliest works on Hebrew poetry; he
asserts the primacy of Hebrew grammar as
found in the Bible over the freer grammar
used by many of the earlier Hebrew poets.

ca. 1140 Rabbi Yehuda Halevi, one of the greatest
Hebrew poets of the Andalusian tradition,
publishes *Kitab al Khazari*, a polemic in
defense of Judaism in the form of a
dialogue between a rabbi and the king of

the Khazars; Halevi writes of Hebrew as the language of the creation (although this book was written in Arabic).

1492 The Jews of Spain are exiled; those who stay in Spain convert to Christianity, but many remain Jews in secret and are subject to the tortures of the Inquisition.

1542 Elijah Levita, author of several Hebrew grammars, publishes first known Yiddish-Hebrew dictionary.

1550 Judah Leone ben Isaac Sommo publishes *Zahut Bedihuta de-Kiddushin*, the oldest Hebrew drama still in existence.

1733 Solomon Zalman ben Judah Loeb ha-Kohen Hanau publishes the Hebrew grammar *Tzohar ha-Tevah*, which will be a major influence on the revival of the Hebrew language.

1755 Publication of Samuel Johnson's *Dictionary*, the first English dictionary to use illustrative quotations. Widely considered to set the standard in dictionaries for the next 150 years.

ca. 1770 Beginning of the *Haskalah* movement among European Jews, which promoted the idea of secular study as a legitimate area of education for Jews.

ca. 1776 Founding of Habad Hasidic movement by Rabbi Shneur Zalman of Lyady.

1783 *Ha-Me'assef*, a Hebrew-language quarterly review, appeared between 1783 and 1797 and between 1809 and 1811.

1819 Founding of the Verein für Kultur und Wissenschaft der Juden, an organization of Jewish intellectuals determined to bring a scientific approach to the study of Judaism; the movement particularly focused on the study of Hebrew.

1834 Yehuda Alkalai of Sarajevo publishes *Shema Israel*, a booklet in which he claims it is unwise to wait for a sign from God to establish Jewish colonies in the Holy Land; he is also an advocate of the use of Hebrew.

1836 David Samuel Luzatto's *Prologomena to a Grammar of the Hebrew Language* published in Padua.

1853 Publication of Abraham Mapu's *Ahavat Tziyyon*, the first novel written in Hebrew.

1856 *Ha-Maggid*, the first Hebrew-language newspaper, is published in Lyc, Prussia, by Eliezer Lipmann Silbermann. David Gordon, editor from 1858 to 1886, is a strong supporter of Jewish nationalism. The paper is read throughout the Jewish world until it ceases publication in 1903.

1858 Birth of Eliezer Ben-Yehuda (né Eliezer Yizhak Perelman) in Luzhky, Lithuania.

1860 Alliance Israélite Universelle, the first international Jewish organization, is founded in Paris to protect

Jews around the world from discrimination and eventually to aid in educating Jews.

1861 Isaac Moses Rumsch publishes a Hebrew translation of *The Adventures of Robinson Crusoe*, based on a German translation.

1862 Rabbi Zevi Hirsch Kalischer publishes *Derishat Tziyyon*, in which he advocates working toward a return to Zion.

1863 Hebrew newspaper *Ha-Havatzelet* begins publication in Jerusalem; closes in 1864 due to controversy within the Jerusalem community, then resumes publication in 1870.

1868 Peretz Smolenskin, Russian Jewish novelist and editor, begins to publish the Hebrew monthly periodical *Ha-Shahar*, an exponent of the Jewish Enlightenment and early Jewish nationalism.

1871 Ben-Yehuda goes to Plotzk to study at Hasidic yeshiva, where he first encounters Jewish Enlightenment grammar; his uncle sends him to yeshiva in Glubokoye, in the Vilna district, to escape influence of his Enlightened teacher.

1876 George Eliot publishes *Daniel Deronda*, a novel that encourages Jews to realize their own national aspirations.

1877 Ben-Yehuda graduates from gymnasium in Dünaburg.

1877–1878 The Russo-Turkish War further inflames nationalist movements across Europe.

1878 Ben-Yehuda goes to Paris to study medicine; there he encounters Jews who have heard Hebrew spoken among Jews in the land of Israel.

That winter, Ben-Yehuda begins to study at the Alliance Israélite Universelle with aim of moving to Palestine and getting a teaching position at the Mikveh Israel school in Tel Aviv.

1879 Ben-Yehuda's article *"She-elah Lohatah"* ("A Burning Question"), in which he makes the case for a national revival in the land of Israel, published under the name E. Ben-Yehuda in Peretz Smolenskin's Hebrew monthly *Ha-Shahar*.

1881 En route to Israel, Ben-Yehuda marries Dvora Jonas, daughter of his teacher Samuel Naphtali Herz Jonas.

In October, Ben-Yehuda and Dvora arrive in Israel, committed to speaking only Hebrew.

ca. 1881 Ben-Yehuda is among the founders of Tehiyyat Yisrael, a society that campaigned for the revival of Hebrew.

1882 Founding of Zikhron Ya'akov, an early Jewish agricultural settlement in the land of Israel.

Ben-Yehuda's son Itamar is born.

1882–1885 Ben-Yehuda works on *Ha-Havatzelet*.

1882–1903 Period of the First Aliyah, or mass immigration, of Jews to Israel, largely from Eastern Europe.

1884 Ben-Yehuda edits *Mevasseret Tziyyon*, a supplement to *Ha-Havatzelet*.

Ben-Yehuda founds weekly Hebrew publication *Ha-Tzvi*; published variously as a weekly, daily, and biweekly under the names *Ha-Tzvi* and *Ha-Or* until 1915.

1889 Ahad Ha-Am, a leading Zionist thinker, begins publishing essays that help shape a modern Jewish philosophy of identity.

1890 Ben-Yehuda cofounds Committee for the Hebrew Language.

1891 Death of Ben-Yehuda's first wife, Dvora.

1895 Ben-Yehuda tried for sedition by Turkey.

1895 Ben-Yehuda excommunicated by Jewish community in Jerusalem.

1896 Theodor Herzl publishes *The Jewish State*.

1897 First Zionist Congress in Basel.

1903–1904 The Hebrew poet Hayyim Nahman Bialik publishes poems *"Al ha-Sh'chitah"* ("On the Slaughter") and *"Be'Ir ha'Haregah"* ("City of Slaughter") in the aftermath of the Kishinev pogrom.

1904–1914 Second Aliyah, largely from Russia.

1908 First Yiddish Language Conference held in Czernowitz, Bukovina, gathers many of the greatest Jewish writers in often contentious discussion of future of Jewish languages.

Discovery of the Gezer Calendar, the oldest known Hebrew writing, dating to the tenth century B.C.E.

1908–1911 Hayyim Nahman Bialik and Yehoshua Hana Ravnitzky publish *Sefer ha-Aggadah*, a Hebrew compilation of classic Jewish midrash, or legends.

1909 Deganyah, a collective settlement, or *kevutzah*, that was the forerunner of the kibbutz movement, founded on Jewish National Fund land south of the Sea of Galilee.

1913–1914 Ben-Yehuda leads opposition to plan by the Hilfsverein der Deutschen Juden (Relief Organization of German Jews) to adopt German as the language of instruction at the Technion in Haifa.

1917 Vladimir Jabotinsky organizes Jewish Legion as part of British Army in World War I; he hopes it will eventually become a Jewish army that will defend the land of Israel.

Death of Ludwik Lazar Zamenhof, Polish contemporary of Ben-Yehuda's, a Zionist and creator of the international language Esperanto.

On November 2, the British government issues the Balfour Declaration, promising "the establishment in Palestine of a national home for the Jewish people."

In December, Ben-Yehuda begins to publish autobiography in serial form in *Ha-Toren*, one of the first Hebrew-language periodicals published in the United States.

1918 First Academy of the Arabic Language founded in Damascus.

1919 Ben-Yehuda returns to Jerusalem, having spent much of World War I in New York because Zionism had been outlawed in Ottoman Empire.

1920 Sir Herbert Samuel, British high commissioner in Palestine, announces at San Remo Conference in April that there will be three official languages in Palestine: English, Arabic, and Hebrew.

1922 Eliezer Ben-Yehuda dies in Jerusalem.

1946 Yehuda Gur, author of several smaller Hebrew dictionaries (including one cowritten with Ben-Yehuda), publishes his most extensive work, *Ha-Milon ha-Ivri*.

1947 Beginning of the discovery of the Dead Sea Scrolls, which are dated to ca. 100 B.C.E.–200 C.E. and provide evidence of the Hebrew language in transition from biblical Hebrew to Mishnaic Hebrew.

1947–1951 Publication of *Ha-Milon ha-Hadash*, a new Hebrew dictionary by Abraham Even-Shoshan.

1948 On May 5, State of Israel declares independence.

1953 The Academy of the Hebrew Language, the governing body of Hebrew language and successor to the Committee for the Hebrew Language, is established by the Knesset.

1959 Completion of the Ben-Yehuda dictionary by Moses Hirsch Segal and Naphtali Herz Tur-Sinai.

1966 S. Y. Agnon is first (and so far only) Hebrew writer to win the Nobel Prize.

2007 Publication of *Milon Ariel*, a new Hebrew dictionary edited by Maya Fruchtman and Daniel Sivan.

ABOUT THE AUTHOR

Ilan Stavans is Lewis-Sebring Professor in Latin American and Latino Culture and Five College Fortieth Anniversary Professor at Amherst College. His books include *The Hispanic Condition* (1995), *The Riddle of Cantinflas* (1997), *On Borrowed Words* (2001), *Spanglish* (2003), *Dictionary Days* (2005), *The Disappearance* (2006), and *Love and Language* (2007). He is the editor of, among other works, *Tropical Synagogues* (1993), *The Oxford Book of Jewish Stories* (1998), *The Poetry of Pablo Neruda* (2003), the three-volume *Isaac Bashevis Singer: Collected Stories* (2004), *The Schocken Book of Modern Sephardic Literature* (2005), and *Cesar Chavez: An Organizer's Tale* (2008). Stavans is the recipient of numerous awards and honors, including a Guggenheim Fellowship, the Latino Hall of Fame Award, Chile's Presidential Medal, the Rubén Darío Medal, and the National Jewish Book Award. Routledge published *The Essential Ilan Stavans* in 2000 and University of Wisconsin Press brought out *Ilan Stavans: Eight Conversations*, by Neal Sokol, in 2004. His oeuvre has been translated into a dozen languages. His stories have been adapted to the theater and screen. Stavans writes a weekly newspaper column syndicated throughout the Spanish-speaking world.